6.95

Economic Growth in China and India 1952-1970

Subramanian Swamy

A Comparative Appraisal

Economic Growth in China and India 1952-1970

The University of Chicago Press
Chicago and London

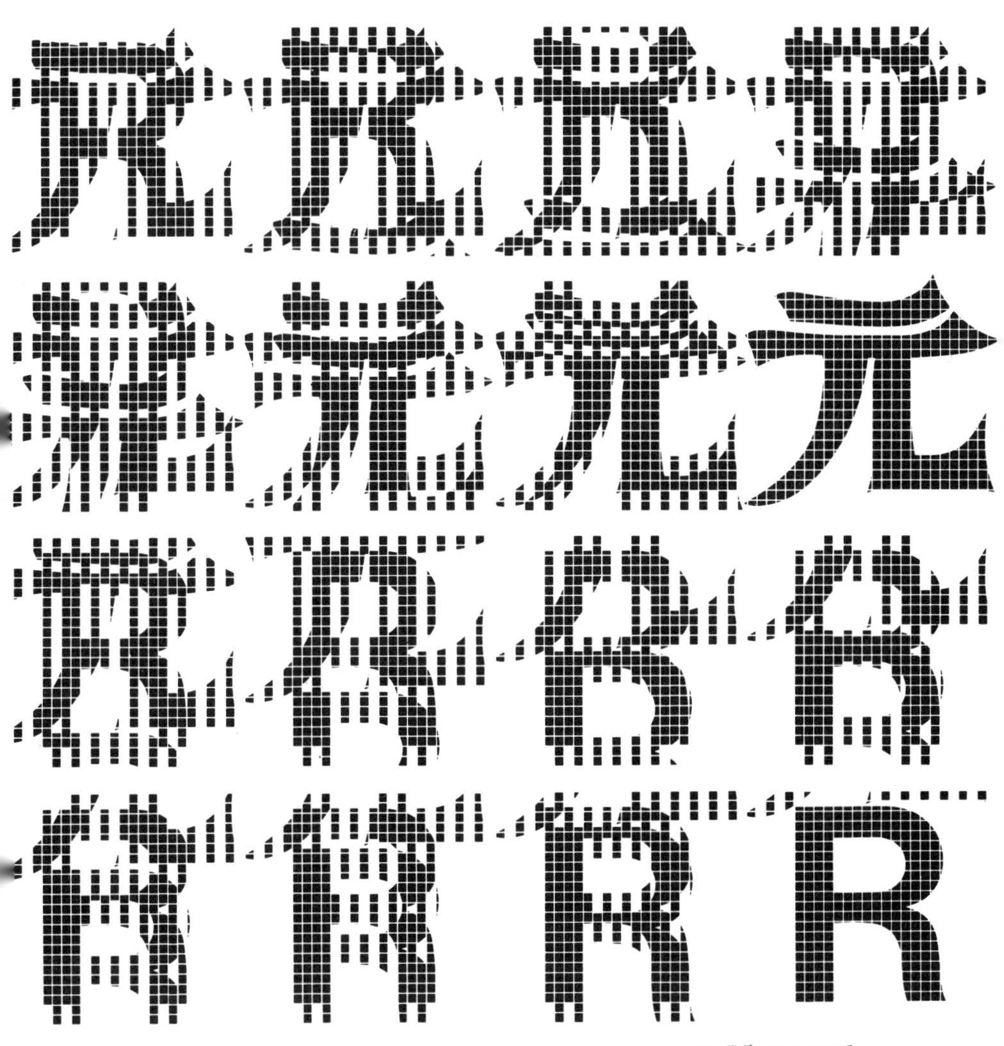

This work also appeared as volume 21, number 4, part 2 (July 1973), of Economic Development and Cultural Change, edited by Bert F. Hoselitz, and published by the University of Chicago Press.

The University of Chicago Press, Chicago 60637
The University of Chicago Press, Ltd., London

Published 1973
Printed in the United States of America

International Standard Book Number: 0-226-78315-4
Library of Congress Catalog Card Number: 72-96344

Contents

Tables

I. Introduction

Introductory Comments

This study is about the economic growth of China and India during the last 20 years. The stable governments that emerged in the late forties in both countries expended great effort toward the transformation of their economies to modern industrial ones. Here I attempt to examine the success they achieved. That this is a hazardous and on occasion speculative undertaking scarcely needs stating. Nevertheless, since economic growth is a quantitative process, I have attempted to establish at least a few important results.

In interpreting the quantitative results, however, there are two major difficulties. The first, for want of data, I shall only mention. There is tacit recognition that most actions that induce growth also impose costs and that the higher income obtained may not be worth the cost. In the context of the China-India comparison, this is a relevant question, for, say, if it turns out that the Chinese growth rate is only $\frac{1}{2}$ percentage point higher than India's rate, one may ask: is this $\frac{1}{2}$ percent worth the costs of social regimentation that the Chinese pay? Alternatively, if the Indian rate is $\frac{1}{2}$ percent higher, is it worth the cost of gross inequality that is permitted in India? I cannot answer this question in any definite sense.

The second difficulty in defining and comparing the economic growth of China and India arises when the meaning of product is considered. Essentially product is defined to convey some appreciation of the economic life of a country. But associated with such a definition are the thorny problems of *scope*, *grossness*, and *valuation*. If we are to understand modern economic growth in China and India, we must measure the magnitudes in terms of the systems of ends, means, and values of the two societies. But these systems are quite diverse. Therefore, the yardstick to be used must be decided.

In China-India comparisons, I propose the evaluation of Chinese concepts in Indian terms. I am, of course, more familiar with the latter, but, more important, a substantive argument supports this decision. One reason for studying two diverse systems, such as China and India, is to judge their relative efficiency in organizing the forces of production in order to raise the standard of living of the people. Since consumer sovereignty and market orientation play a greater role in the Indian economy, concepts evaluated in Indian terms are likely to have a wider significance for the measurement of living standards. For example, certain consumer services are excluded from product according to the Chinese concept but included in the Indian concept. From the point of view of the criterion set out above, it appears more logical to include these services and evaluate product according to Indian concepts (which incidentally are derived from the system of national accounts used by the United Nations). However, I do not apply this evaluation mechanically, and, in fact, in some special situations it was deemed more appropriate to tailor the Indian concept to conform with the Chinese concept.

Problems of Scope

There is little need to deal extensively with problems regarding the estimation of national income of China because a considerable literature is available.[1] The Chinese definition of product is that of material product measured in net terms and at constant market prices, whereas the Indian definition is that of national income (including services) in net terms at factor costs. I quote four Chinese economists to clarify the definition used in China:

> Po I-po: "The national income is the total value of production of industry, agriculture, building industry, plus the value created by transport and commercial workers, i.e., total value of production minus depreciation charges of the means of production. In other words, it is the net value of production."[2]
>
> Niou Jong-hwang: "National income is made thus of the total production value of the national economy after deducting the amount of material consumption (the consumption of production means)."[3]
>
> Yang Boh: "National income represents material wealth created by various material production agencies in society during a fixed period, and those material production agencies, according to our present classification of our national economy, include industry, agriculture, building industry, commerce (including restaurant business), communications, transportation, postal and telecommunication services."[4]
>
> Lu Guang: "National income is here taken to mean the value-added to the country's material wealth to productive activities and those serving production over a given period. The national income is thus the gross social product minus the means of production consumed in creating the new wealth."[5]

[1] See, e.g., Shigeru Ishikawa, *National Income and Capital Formation in Mainland China* (Tokyo: Institute of Asian Economic Affairs, 1965); T. C. Liu and K. C. Yeh, *The Economy of the Chinese Mainland* (Princeton, N.J.: Princeton University Press, 1965); Li Choh-ming, *Economic Development of Communist China* (Berkeley: University of California Press, 1959).

[2] *Documents of the Chinese Communist Party Eighth Congress* (Peking: People's Publishing House, 1957).

[3] *Accumulation and Consumption in the National Income of China* (Peking: China Youth Publication Institute, 1957), chap. 2.

[4] "A Study of the Distribution of National Income," *Jing Jih Yan Jiou* (Peking), no. 6, December 17, 1957.

[5] "China's National Income," *Peking Review*, no. 6, April 8, 1958.

From these four definitions, we may deduce several things about the Chinese definition of national income. The primary focus is on the material product broadly defined to include services which serve production. For example, the part of transport and postal and telecommunication serving material production is included, but the component serving consumers is not. All commercial trading agencies are included. These subsectors of service are easily identified from Chinese publications. But in the case of a laundry washing factory uniforms, or a doctor treating factory casualties, the official Chinese practice is unclear. It seems reasonable to conjecture that these services are treated like transport services and are included if they serve production.

Second, the national income is net in two senses: (1) depreciation, or rather obsolescence, is subtracted; and (2) cost of production is also deducted. It is necessary to bear this in mind because when Chinese economists talk of "means of production consumed" they refer to both items.

Third, all products, whether "marketed" or produced for own consumption, are included. The nonmarketed portion is evaluated, according to Niou, on a "representative basis." This vague term presumably means that ad hoc methods are adopted. The reliability of such methods is, of course, in doubt.

Fourth, pure trading agencies are included, and their contribution is obtained simply by multiplying the difference between retail and wholesale price by the quantity. This means that, ultimately, national income is evaluated in retail prices in China. The international standards are different: the term "market price" implies those prices at which the goods and services were bought or could have been bought, and not necessarily retail prices.[6] Also, "trading agency" in China means a change of "ownership," and no value is added to the product because of the transfer. In other words, more is included than is standard international practice.

Fifth, the Chinese product is at market price, never in factor cost.

Thus, the Chinese and Indian concepts of national income differ in five respects: (1) certain services to the consumers, for example, laundry but not restaurant services, are excluded in China but not in India; (2) utilities serving consumers are included in India but not in China; (3) banking and insurance are excluded in China but included in India; (4) services of professors, musicians, etc., are excluded in China but not in India; (5) all production, whether exchanged or not, is included in China but not in India; the amount of nonprimary production performed by producers outside their own trade and consumed by themselves is excluded. In effect, China's concept of production is wider than that of India. In practice, this difference is even larger: India excludes even *own-trade* nonprimary production if only because of lack of data.

[6] See *A System of National Accounts and Supporting Tables* (New York: United Nations, 1964), p. 8.

Problems of Netness and Grossness

Netness implies deducting two items: (1) all costs of production, and (2) obsolescence. The first item is relatively straightforward, but the estimation of obsolescence is quite difficult. It is based on the judgment of the national income statistician. It is his estimation of the economic life of fixed capital and is quantitatively larger, never less, than physical depreciation if a country is experiencing modern economic growth. India follows the standard U.N. practice; economic life is estimated, and straight-line obsolescence is taken. Unforeseen obsolescence is written off as a capital loss. But given the tax exemptions associated with economic expansion and modernization, this write-off is rarely necessary. In China, as in many other socialist countries, the tendency is to understate obsolescence primarily by overstating the physical life of the equipment. Investment, in turn, is overstated, but little can be done about it because of lack of data. Therefore, some caution must be exercised in interpreting investment data.

Summary

Table 1 indicates the main differences in scope and netness.

TABLE 1

TREATMENT OF SPECIFIC PROBLEMS OF NATIONAL ACCOUNTS, CHINA AND INDIA

Item	China	India
Scope of primary activity	All major produce such as rice, wheat, etc., as well as minor agricultural produce	Standard U.N.
Services of general government assets	Uncertain	No imputation
Factor income from abroad	Excluded	Investment income only; other factor incomes are included with non-factor services
Valuation of primary product	Retail prices	Wholesale prices prevailing in the primary market
Provisions of capital consumption	Underestimated	Standard U.N.
Valuation of provisions for capital consumption	Book value	Book value generally, but replacement cost basis in agriculture
Change in stocks	Standard	Standard
Valuation of total	Net, market prices	Net, factor cost

This study contains most of the quantitative work on agriculture, industry, and national income. The main purposes are to establish a consistent series of value-added figures for agriculture and industry, establish the proper weights for addition of the net value-added figures, and estimate the growth rates of China and India on the basis of these consistent series.

II. Agriculture and Its Contribution to Growth

Introduction

Agriculture makes three types of contribution to economic growth: (1) product contribution, (2) market contribution, and (3) factor contribution. The product contribution predominates in most discussions of agricultural performance. It is simply the contribution to the total output through its sectoral product. By denoting the rate of growth as r, the agricultural sector as subscript a, and the nonagricultural sector as subscript b, we have the following equation:

$$r = w_a r_a + w_b r_b, \qquad (1)$$

where w is the weight of the sector measured as a fraction of total product.

Thus the contribution of the agriculture sector to the overall rate of growth, expressed as a percentage of the total rate of growth, equals $(w_a r_a / r) \times 100$ and is termed the *product contribution* of the agriculture sector.

Agriculture makes a *market contribution* by (1) purchasing either current inputs or producer goods from other sectors, mostly from the manufacturing sector; (2) purchasing consumer goods to satisfy increasing needs; (3) selling some of its product ("marketed surplus") to pay for its purchases or to accumulate capital. The trends are important because they indicate the technological transformation of the agricultural sector and its modernization. Thus manufactured chemical fertilizers, machinery, and mechanical power replace less efficient inputs (organic fertilizer, draught animals, and wooden ploughs) which are produced *within* the agriculture sector. In order to pay for these purchases, the marketed output of agriculture has to be increased. Thus the *market contribution* of agriculture is an important strategic variable which makes a *structural contribution* to modern economic growth.

The third type, *factor contribution* of agriculture, is also important to economic growth, especially in countries with economic planning, such as China and India. This type of contribution occurs when resources are transferred from agriculture to the other sectors. The resources are, of course, capital and labor. Capital is transferred either *voluntarily*, that is, by lending or investing in the nonagricultural sector, or *involuntarily*, that is, ordinarily through direct and indirect taxation. The experience of most rapidly developing countries, for example, Japan and the USSR, shows that this type of contribution is crucial. The transfer of workers also means a transfer of capital because each migrant is of working age and represents investments of the agriculture sector in rearing, education, and training.

Because of the paucity of data in China and India, market and factor contributions are more difficult to estimate than product contribution. Furthermore, once estimated, they raise some fundamental questions as to policy aspects of economic planning. Since this study is concerned primarily with the establishment of reliable basic series of outputs, only the product contribution is considered in this volume.

Foodgrains Output in China and India, 1952–70

The first problem is that of data. For India, a large body of information is available, but suspected underestimation in the output figures for the early fifties needed investigation. The problem for China is much more difficult. In the first place, since 1960 the Chinese have not published official absolute figures for foodgrains output. However, estimates of several reputable "China scholars" are available.

Since available estimates by Sinologists of foodgrains output for 1958–65 appear to have some internal contradictions, I have prepared alternative estimates. This alternative series incorporates figures provided by Chinese officials to a Pakistani delegation that went to China in August 1965 (to study the communes).[7] The information used here was given in response to a questionnaire submitted to the officials of the Ministry of Agriculture and the Bureau of Commune Management.

The foodgrain production statistics given to the delegation are in two parts. For 1952–57, they are the official published figures and do not differ significantly from the estimates of the China scholars. However, the output figures for 1958–65 are substantially different. A test of internal validity was made, which suggests that my output series is more acceptable in terms of internal consistency than the others.[8]

The OSB Grain Output Series for China, 1952–70

The estimates of grain production, presented in table 2, are basically official Chinese. For 1952–65, output data are those supplied to the Pakistani delegation. The 1966–67 figures have been obtained by collating official or semi-official Chinese statements. The 1970 figure is from Edgar Snow's interview with Chou En-lai in early 1971.[9]

[7] Shahid J. Burki was a member of this three-man delegation. For details, see Burki, *A Study of Chinese Communes*, East Asia Monographs (Cambridge, Mass.: Harvard University Press, 1969).

[8] See Appendix A; see also R. M. Field, "How Much Grain Does Communist China Produce?" *China Quarterly*, no. 33 (January-March 1968), pp. 98–101.

[9] *Epoca* (Italy), February 28, 1971, quoted in *Times of India*, March 19, 1971.

TABLE 2

FOODGRAINS OUTPUT IN CHINA

Year	Output Unprocessed (MMT) (1)	Output Processed (MMT) (2)	Annual Change (%) (3)	Year End Population (Millions) (4)	Output per Capita* (Kg/Yr) (5)
1952.......	154.4	123.5	...	568.9	217.1
1953.......	156.9	125.5	1.3	582.6	215.4
1954.......	160.9	128.7	2.3	594.2	216.6
1955.......	174.8	139.8	9.0	607.3	230.2
1956.......	182.5	146.0	4.1	620.6	235.3
1957.......	185.5	148.4	1.0	634.3	234.0
1958.......	215.2	172.2	14.0	648.3	265.6
1959.......	192.7	154.2	−7.5	662.5	232.8
1960.......	161.3	129.0	−19.3	677.0	190.5
1961.......	189.2	151.4	20.8	691.9	218.8
1962.......	203.8	163.0	3.8	707.1	230.5
1963.......	218.9	175.1	7.4	722.7	242.3
1964.......	237.8	190.2	8.6	738.6	257.5
1965.......	240.0	192.0	0.9	745.8	254.4
1966.......	220.0	176.0	−8.3	771.4	228.2
1967.......	231.0	184.8	5.0	788.4	234.1
1968.......	n.a.	n.a.	n.a.	805.7	n.a.
1969.......	n.a.	n.a.	n.a.	823.4	n.a.
1970.......	240.0	192.0	n.a.	841.5	228.2

SOURCES.—Col. 1: 1952—*Ten Great Years* [Wei Dah de Shyr Nian] (Peking: Statistical Publishing House, 1959). 1953–64—Subramanian Swamy and Shahid J. Burki, "Foodgrains Output in the People's Republic of China," *China Quarterly*, no. 41 (January-March 1970). 1965 and 1970—The estimate for 1965 (given in ibid.) was 258 MMT. However, Chou En-lai told Edgar Snow (*Epoca*, February 28, 1971) that the 1970 figure was 240 MMT, and Radio Peking claimed that "grain output last [1970] was the highest since the founding of China" (*Government of India Monitoring Service*, February 24, 1971). Hence this estimate was scaled down to 240 MMT, keeping in view Vice-Minister of Agriculture Wu Chen's statement that the 1965 grain output was larger than the 1964 grain output (see "Excellent Situation in Chinese Agriculture," *Jing Jih Daw Baw*, March 28, 1966, pp. 12–13). 1966–67—By collating statements made by Anna Louise Strong, "Letter from China," January 15, 1968, Hsieh Fu-chih, "Fight Self, Repudiate Revisionism," trans. in *Survey of Current Mainland Press*, no. 4076; and by Chou En-lai in *Tzu-Liao Chuan-chi*, trans. in *Survey of Current Mainland Press*, nos. 4080 and 4154. Col. 2: Col. 1 × 0.80. Col. 4: The 1953 figures extrapolated by 2.2 percent per year.

NOTE.—n.a. = not available.

* Cols. 2 ÷ 4.

For 1952–57, the figures are virtually the same as those published by the State Statistical Bureau and only slightly higher than those accepted by most Western Sinologists. However, for the year after 1959, the figures are higher and grow more rapidly than any Sinologist's estimate. To distinguish this series from others it is labeled OSB (Official-Swamy-Burki estimates).[10] Two aspects of the OSB estimates have been criticized by Field.[11] First, he argues they imply that, if the Chinese government had held the per capita consumption constant at the 1957/58 level from 1962/63 on, by 1965 the government would have accumulated a surplus of 50.8

[10] For details, see Subramanian Swamy and Shahid J. Burki, "Foodgrains Output in the People's Republic of China," *China Quarterly*, no. 41 (January-March 1970).

[11] R. M. Field, "Chinese Grain Production," *China Quarterly*, no. 46 (April-June 1971).

million metric tons (MMT) and would not have needed any imports. The Chinese did import 4–5 million metric tons of grain annually. This criticism is unjustified. In the first place we have no reason to assume that the Chinese would rigidly clamp consumption to the 1957/58 level, although we grant that some consumption control was essential to replace grain stocks that had been depleted by 1962.[12] But with a gradually escalating consumption level (which is necessary if the Chinese officials are at least serious about their objective of 400 kilograms of grain per person), the Chinese could still accumulate sufficient stocks. Since the transport network was overloaded, weak, and costly, simultaneous and continual imports of grain were desirable. Second, Premier Chou En-lai in his 1971 interview with Snow claimed that China had a stock of 40 million metric tons but continued to import wheat because China exports rice and also donates grain to North Vietnam and other countries.[13]

Field's second criticism is based on its implications for yield per hectare. As his calculations show, the OSB estimates imply that during 1957–64 the increase in production of 26.9 percent was accounted for by a 6.5 percent increase in sown area and a 20.4 percent increase in yield per hectare. Field questions this. Available input data suggested that a rise of 2.7 percent annually is hardly spectacular, since attention and resources were shifted toward the agricultural sector after the failure of the Great Leap Forward. During this period, chemical fertilizer production grew 440 percent, that is, from 0.94 million metric tons in 1957 to 4.97 in 1964. Use of irrigation pumps, pesticides, multiple cropping, and better commune organization grew at corresponding rates. Furthermore, during the same period the rate of increase in yield per hectare in India was even higher.

The OSB estimates are the highest for grain production in China. As already stated, our major conclusions would only be strengthened if lower estimates had been used. Moreover, our estimates contradict only one[14] of the official statements on grain production made from time to time.

Scope of Foodgrains Output

Two problems of scope had to be resolved before the outputs of India and of China could be compared. First, China's grain output is unprocessed

[12] At the beginning of 1960/61, the Chinese had a stock of 26.1 MMT of grain.

[13] The Field estimate of 50.8 MMT grain surplus by 1965 was based on a preliminary OSB estimate for 1965. The latter was 258 MMT but has been revised to 240 MMT. This revision, coupled with the shortfalls during the Cultural Revolution, makes Chou's 40 MMT claim plausible.

[14] The single contradictory statement is that of Mao Tse-tung in 1961. But Mao has made other numerical statements which are off the mark; e.g., in 1964, he claimed that the population of China was much less than 680 million (Edgar Snow, "Interview with Mao," *New Republic*, February 27, 1965, p. 20). That officials in an interview claim a certain figure does not bind them to it. They are open to revision after firmer estimates are available. E.g., Chou En-lai appeared to change his view on the 1967 output from October 1967 to February 1968.

output, that is, before husking or milling. There is no agreement on the extraction rates that should be used. Official Chinese publications are not explicit. The most authoritative source states that "computation shall be based on the following methods: all grains should be calculated on the basis of the original grain (corn shall, however, be computed on shelled corn basis); potatoes shall be converted into grain value at the rate of four *jin* [1 *jin* = $\frac{1}{2}$ kg] of potatoes to one *jin* of grain"[15] but says nothing about extraction rates. Nor does an authoritative source[16] for India give the extraction rates used. Table 3 presents some commonly used extraction

TABLE 3

Extraction Ratio in Various Countries (%)

Crop	China (1)	India (2)	Taiwan (3)	Japan (4)
Rice	0.72	0.67	0.76	0.80
Wheat	0.85	0.90	0.75	0.75
Misc. grain	0.92	0.70	n.a.	0.69
Potatoes.	1.00(0.92)	1.00	n.a.	1.00
Foodgrains	0.80	0.72	n.a.	0.83

Sources.—Col. 1: *Current Scene*, January 22, 1962 (the overall extraction ratio compares well with Ishikawa's estimate of 0.809). Cols. 2–4: *Technical Comparison Factors for Agricultural Commodities* (Rome: UNFAO, 1968).

ratios. Since Indian figures are for husked output,[17] the problem relates only to China, whose output is weighed before husking. To simplify this minor problem, I have deflated the Chinese figures *by an average* of 20 percent (see table 2).

Second, since the Chinese output figures include potatoes and Indian figures do not, should they be included or excluded for both countries? The selection of either alternative is significant for China and unimportant for India. For China, exclusion of the grain equivalent of potatoes implies an 18 percent reduction in the output of processed foodgrains, whereas for India exclusion implies at most a 1.5 percent reduction. But because the focus on foodgrains production stems from the consumption viewpoint, and potatoes do form a significant portion of the Chinese consumption basket, one could argue that they should be included for China and retain comparability for India also.

But the problem does not end there. One could argue that, by shifting a certain fraction of her acreage under miscellaneous grain to potatoes, India could increase output significantly. To illustrate, the yield per hectare in India of miscellaneous grain is 5.0 quintals per hectare and that of *grain-equivalent* potatoes is 18.0 quintals per hectare. If 25 percent of the

[15] *Handbook of Agricultural Statistical Work* (Peking: Statistical Publication House, 1956), pp. 20–21.

[16] *Handbook of Agriculture* (New Delhi: Indian Council of Agricultural Research, 1967).

[17] Note, however, that the 72 percent extraction rate for India is much lower than 80 percent for China. Also henceforth we use the term "processed" for husked.

miscellaneous grain production were shifted to potatoes, foodgrains production immediately would rise roughly (1.8–0.5) × 15 million, or 19.5 million metric tons. In this situation, the distribution of land by crops would be similar to that in China. Thus, about 15 percent of the output difference between China and India is directly attributable to production of potatoes.

Rate of Growth of Foodgrains Output in China and India, 1952–70

We resorted to the arguments of consumer sovereignty and included potatoes in their grain-equivalent form. Table 4, which summarizes the

TABLE 4

PROCESSED FOODGRAINS OUTPUT, CHINA AND INDIA

Year	Output (MMT)		Annual Change (%)		Ratio Cols. 2 to 1
	China (1)	India (2)	China (3)	India (4)	(5)
1952	123.5	52.7	...	...	0.43
1953	125.5	59.9	1.3	13.7	0.48
1954	128.7	70.6	2.3	17.9	0.55
1955	129.8	68.8	9.0	−2.6	0.49
1956	146.0	67.7	4.1	−1.6	0.46
1957	148.4	70.6	1.0	4.3	0.48
1958	172.2	65.1	14.0	−7.8	0.38
1959	154.2	78.0	−7.5	19.8	0.51
1960	129.0	77.7	−19.3	−0.1	0.60
1961	151.4	83.0	20.8	8.1	0.55
1962	163.0	83.5	3.8	0.6	0.51
1963	175.1	79.6	7.4	−4.7	0.45
1964	190.2	81.1	8.6	1.9	0.43
1965	192.0	90.3	0.9	11.3	0.47
1966	176.0	73.2	−8.3	−18.9	0.42
1967	184.8	76.2	5.0	4.1	0.41
1968	n.a.	96.6	n.a.	26.8	n.a.
1969	n.a.	96.0	n.a.	−0.6	n.a.
1970	192.0	102.0	n.a.	6.3	0.53
1971	n.a.	107.0	n.a.	4.9	n.a.

SOURCES.—Col. 1: Table 2. Col. 2: 1952–71—*Bulletin on Food Statistics* (New Delhi: Directorate of Economics and Statistics, Ministry of Food, Agriculture, Community Development and Cooperation, February 1972 and earlier issues).

results, suggests the following conclusions. First, India's output was generally 40–50 percent of China's output. Over time, while considerable cyclic movement is apparent, this ratio increased. Second, the year-to-year rate of growth appeared to fluctuate much more for India than for China. This is, of course, to be expected in a market-oriented economy. In India output declined seven times, in China only three. Third, the *drop* in output in China was of catastrophic proportions, although only occurring in three out of sixteen years: in 1959, 1960, and 1966 (7.5 percent, 19.3 percent, and 8.3 percent, respectively).[18] Behind these severe declines are the well-known events of Great Leap, Drought, and Cultural Revolution.

[18] According to estimates of Western Sinologists, the drop in output in 1966 was relatively negligible.

In India the output declines have not been severe, except during 1965–66 when the poor harvests were a direct result of an unprecedented drought.

The overall growth rates are sensitive to the choice of the terminal year. The years 1967–71 are excellent years for India but not for China. On the other hand, 1965–66 are years of poor output in both countries. One way of resolving this problem is to consider as a terminal year that year which is good for both countries, as 1965 when both China and India had larger outputs than in any previous year. India passed this peak in 1967–68, 1968–69, 1969–70, whereas China did not regain the 1965 peak until 1970. *Any lengthening of the time series would therefore be favorable to India.* That, however, leads to statistical complications, since the rate of growth estimated with 1965 as the terminal year is biased upward. One solution to this problem is to use an average, with the years covered in averaging selected to remove the cyclic variations. A natural period would be 5 years, since both China and India have 5-year plans. However, a 5-year period while acceptable for some sets of years is not appropriate for others. In India, for instance, the monsoon cycle has generally varied in the neighborhood of 3 years, not 5. In China the 5-year plans have been abandoned for political reasons. Hence, the averages adopted here have varying periods: for the rates of growth I used a 5-year average centered on 1954, a 3-year average centered on 1958, and a 5-year average centered on 1963. These rates of growth are presented in table 5.

TABLE 5

RATE OF GROWTH OF FOODGRAINS OUTPUT, CHINA AND INDIA (% PER YEAR)

Period	China	India
1952–56 to 1957–59	4.3	2.7
1957–59 to 1961–65	1.4	3.2
1961–65 to 1970	1.5	2.9
1952–56 to 1961–65	2.6	3.0
1952–56 to 1970	2.2	2.9

SOURCE.—Table 4.

Several observations can be made. First, for the period of 1952–65, the Chinese rate of growth of foodgrains is only 2.6 percent per year and somewhat lower than the rate for India. Second, extension of the time period would strengthen this observation. Since the rate of growth in China during 1961–70 was 1.5 percent per year, extension of the period to 1970 lowers the rate to 2.2 percent for the entire period 1952–70. The rate of growth in India is virtually unaffected by the extension of the period. Third, for two of the three subperiods, the rate of growth is higher in India than in China. The Chinese rate is higher only during 1952–59. Fourth, the rate of growth in China drops from 4.3 percent in the first period to 1.4 and 1.5 percent in the second and third periods. In India, the trends are mixed: the rate rises from 2.5 percent to 3.2 percent and then drops to 2.9 percent. While this deceleration reflects the sluggishness of agriculture during the sixties (which necessitated large-scale imports), the periodization employed above does hide important output trends. For example, the foodgrains output of China is almost the same in 1958 as in 1963; the 1965 output is the same as that of 1970. In India the rate of growth since 1967 has been much higher than the trend rate (hence the name "Green Revolution").

Obviously the differences in output levels of growth rates are assignable to inputs and cropping pattern. I shall attempt, therefore, in the section below, to estimate their quantitative significance. The calculation is carried out in three steps. First, the differences due to cropping pattern are calculated. Second, the contribution of inputs to differences in output, crop by crop, is estimated. Finally, the differences in growth rates are broken down into differences in the rate of input application.

Output of Foodgrains by Crop, China and India, 1952–65

The structure of foodgrains output in terms of rice, wheat, miscellaneous grain, and potatoes differs between the two countries (table 6). In both

TABLE 6

FOODGRAINS: OUTPUT, ACREAGE, AND YIELD PER HECTARE BY CROPS, CHINA AND INDIA

PERIOD	RICE		WHEAT		MISC. GRAIN		GRAIN-EQUIV POTATOES		FOODGRAINS	
	China	India	China	India	China	India	China	India	China	India
1952–56:										
Q	53.4	24.9	18.3	7.9	47.8	30.4	16.7	0.8	136.3	63.9
A	30.0	30.7	26.3	10.7	51.6	63.9	8.3	0.4	116.2	105.8
Q/A	1.8	0.8	0.7	0.7	0.9	0.5	2.0	2.0	1.2	0.6
1957–59:										
Q	65.6	28.4	21.3	9.1	49.9	32.9	24.1	0.9	160.9	71.2
A	32.5	32.6	27.1	12.6	47.6	65.8	13.6	0.5	120.8	112.2
Q/A	2.0	0.9	0.8	0.7	1.1	0.5	1.8	1.8	1.3	0.6
1961–65:										
Q	70.3	35.6	21.1	11.2	61.2	35.6	22.8	1.0	175.4	83.5
A	33.2	35.1	25.1	13.4	54.0	67.9	13.9	0.5	126.3	117.0
Q/A	2.1	1.0	0.8	0.8	1.1	0.5	1.6	2.0	1.4	0.7

SOURCES.—Tables A5–A8.

NOTE.—Q = output in MMT, A = area in million hectares, Q/A = yield in tons per hectare.

countries, rice accounts for about 40 percent and wheat for about 13 percent of the total. However, differences arise in the case of potatoes and that of miscellaneous grain. In China, potatoes, in grain-equivalent form, account for about 14 percent of output, while in India they are less than 1 percent. The share of miscellaneous grain is much higher in India (46 percent) than in China (33 percent).

Since both China and India are predominantly rice-consuming countries, rice technology is an important determining factor in any analysis of the growth potential of foodgrains.

Sources of Differences in Foodgrains Output, China and India

Since total acreage sown in China is not very different from that in India, differences in output reflect different yields per hectare. The acreage under the rice crop is about 32 million hectares in both countries, but the output of rice is more than twice as large in India as in China. The same is true for miscellaneous grain. For wheat and potatoes, however, the yields per hectare are about the same, but outputs of these two crops are significantly different because of the different acreages. The overall result is that the yield per hectare of foodgrains in China is about twice that in India.

Differences Due to Output Structure

To what extent can the output differences between the two countries be assigned to acreage and to yield per hectare? With equation (2), this question is easy to answer:

$$Q^1 - Q^2 = \sum_{j=1}^{N} (a_j^1 - a_j^2)q_j^2 + \sum_{J=1}^{N} a_j^1(q_j^1 - q_j^2), \quad (2)$$

where Q^1 = total foodgrains output of the ith country in million metric tons; a_j^i = acreage under jth crop, in ith country, in hectares; q_j^i = yield per hectare, in metric tons per hectare; $i = 1$ for China, 2 for India; N = number of crops, here $N = 4$.

Table 7 demonstrates that the difference between Chinese and Indian foodgrain outputs is due partly to a larger absolute acreage under wheat and potatoes in China, and partly to a higher yield per hectare in China of rice and miscellaneous grain. The first factor (acreage) is the less important one, accounting for only 26 percent of the total difference in output.

TABLE 7

FOODGRAINS OUTPUT DIFFERENCES BY CROP, CHINA AND INDIA, 1952–65

Source	MMT
Due to differences in acreage:	
Rice	−1.03
Wheat	+10.63
Miscellaneous grain	−7.31
Grain-equivalent potatoes	+23.47
Total due to acreage	+25.76
Due to differences in yield per hectare:	
Rice	+34.41
Wheat	+0.09
Miscellaneous grain	+31.00
Grain-equivalent potatoes	+0.18
Total due to yield per hectare	+65.68
Explained difference	+91.44
Observed difference	+91.00

SOURCES.—Table 6 and eq. (2). Figures represent the excess of Chinese output over Indian output.

Furthermore, it is largely due to the difference in acreage under potatoes, already discussed. The second factor, higher yield per hectare in China, is subjected to a closer examination.

Differences Due to Direct Input

An input-output relationship generally satisfies some regularity condition, such as continuity or differentiability:

$$Q = f(x_1, \ldots, x_5, X), \tag{3}$$

where Q = output, and $x_1, \ldots, x_5$ represent direct inputs. The X is a proxy for all other inputs and is generally estimated as a residual since it cannot be explicitly quantified.

If superscripts 1 and 2 are appended to denote China and India, respectively, then, using y as the input available for India,

$$Q^1 - Q^2 = f^1(x_1, \ldots, x_5, X) - f^2(y_1, \ldots, y_5, Y) \tag{4}$$

or

$$Q^1 - Q^2 = \sum_{j=1}^{5} x_j \left(\frac{\partial f^1}{\partial x_j} - \frac{\partial f^2}{\partial y_j}\right) + \sum_{j=1}^{5} \frac{\partial f^2}{\partial y_j}(x_j - y_j),$$

assuming returns to scale.[19]

That is, the difference in foodgrains output is a weight sum of two terms: (1) difference in marginal productivities of inputs, and (2) difference in level of inputs applied. Since it has already been noted that the main difference in output between China and India is due to yield per hectare, equation (4) is considered only in terms of per hectare units.[20]

The following observations are based on table 8. First, the total "explained" difference of 91.02 million metric tons is quite close to the "observable" difference of 91.00 million metric tons. Second, the major factor in the output differences is the yield per hectare, which contributes 79.6 percent of the total difference. In one sense, this finding only emphasizes the one made above. In another sense, it is more profound, implying

[19] We have little evidence to prove this assumption, especially for Chinese agriculture. But I have based it on commune data (see Subramanian Swamy, "Institutional Change and Productivity in Chinese Agriculture" in *Structure and Development of Asian Economies* [Tokyo: Japan Economic Research Center, 1968]).

[20] Differences in the rates of growth in output can be written as follows:

$$\dot{Q}^1/Q^1 - \dot{Q}^2/Q^2 = \sum_{i=1}^{5} (n_i^1 - n_i^2)\frac{\dot{y}_i}{y_i} + \sum_{i=1}^{5} n_i^1 \left(\frac{\dot{x}_i}{x_i} - \frac{\dot{y}_i}{y_i}\right), \tag{5}$$

where n_i = elasticity of output with respect to ith input. Thus, the difference in rates of growth is a weighted sum of the differences in the output elasticity of inputs and the rate of growth of inputs. However, we do not have sufficient data to estimate the components of this equation.

TABLE 8
OUTPUT DIFFERENCES DUE TO INPUT AND PRODUCTIVITY, CHINA AND INDIA, 1952–64

Source	Contribution (MMT)	%
Due to differences in input levels:		
Area	11.58	12.7
Horsepower	0.30	0.0
Chemical fertilizer	7.02	7.7
Total difference	18.90	20.4
Due to differences in productivity of inputs:		
Area	72.49	79.6
Horsepower	−0.05	0.0
Chemical fertilizer	−0.42	0.0
Total difference	72.02	79.6
Total	91.02	100.0

SOURCES.—Eq. (5) and tables A10 and A11.

that land, *after allowing for differences in input levels of power and chemical fertilizer*, is (still) more productive in China than in India. This may reflect a greater use of natural or organic fertilizer in China (4.7 MMT vs. 2.0 MMT in India), a higher proportion of land under irrigation (34 percent in China vs. 18 percent in India), and more fertile land used for foodgrain production in China than in India (in India, more fertile and irrigated lands go to the production of "cash" crops, e.g., sugar cane, jute, cotton, etc.). Third, the second observation implies that the absolute difference between China and India could be reduced at reasonable cost if India would use the available organic manure more extensively, would shift part of the acreage under cash crops to the production of foodgrains, and generally improve and extend minor irrigation works. Interestingly enough, the Chinese agricultural strategy has emphasized precisely these traditional input applications. Fourth, the differences in input *level* account for less than a quarter of the output difference between China and India. Here again, the principal contributor is acreage. While both countries have more or less exhausted the available cultivable acreage (more true of China), China has a much larger multiple cropping index (see tables A10 and A11). India could easily close the gap in output by increasing the number of crops sown per year. Consequently, India's potential to expand the intensity of cultivation is significantly larger than that of China.

Nonfoodgrains Output by Crop, China and India, 1952–65

Data on nonfoodgrain crops are quite poor, although they may be slightly better in India. Information is so scarce that even inferences regarding the weakness of the data are not possible. Consequently, official data have been used as given. We can only hope that suggestions based on these data will not be far wrong. Any definitive statement must wait for more complete information. Because of the importance of nonfoodgrain crops, some observations, albeit preliminary, must be made. One further point: the data series has been terminated at 1965, a good year for both countries. A more recent terminal data would improve the relative performance of India.

The pattern of land utilization for nonfoodgrain production is basically the same in China and India: about 20–25 percent of the total sown area is under nonfoodgrain crops. Of this ratio, 11–15 percent is under oilseeds (if one includes soybeans), about 5–8 percent is under "other crops" (mostly sugarcane, tobacco, and vegetables). No particular trend is visible in any of these figures except that during the drought period in China, 1960–61, and probably during the Cultural Revolution significant acreage was shifted from "cash" crop cultivation to grain growing.[21] The proportion of area under foodgrains in China rose from 76.9 percent in 1957 to 84.2 percent in 1961–62. In later years this percentage began to decline again. Second, total nonfoodgrain output is about the same in India as in China. Since acreage under nonfoodgrain crops is 50 percent higher in India than in China, despite the higher yield per hectare in China, total output is approximately the same in both countries. However, the trends are different. Both total output and yields per hectare have grown faster in India, and by the end of the period India's output exceeded China's by a substantial margin. Third, the rates of growth of nonfoodgrain crops provide some interesting insights into the performance of agriculture in China and India.

From table 9 it is evident that, for the nonfoodgrain group, India's performance has been relatively better than that of China. Although the overall rate of growth of nonfoodgrain output in India has only been 2.9 percent, the corresponding rate for China has been negative. The main reason for the Chinese negative rate of growth is the rapid decline in acreage under nonfoodgrains, especially after 1960. For example, acreage under oilseeds (including soybeans) declined at an annual rate of 8.4 percent since 1958. Three factors help to explain this decline. First, since 1960, the Chinese government has been shifting acreage from nonfoodgrain crop to foodgrains. This policy was established after the severe drought of 1960–61 caused a drop in output of foodgrains from 215 million metric tons (in 1958) to about 160 (see table 2). Second, the price policy in China with regard to oilseeds has been highly irrational. For example, for edible oil Chinese peasants paid double for oilseeds, which was a deterrent to production.[22] Third, yield-raising inputs—as fertilizer,

[21] According to Radio Peking (March 10, 1970, monitored by All India Radio), the acreage under cotton declined from 1965 to 1968. Radio Peking explicitly states that the rate of growth of cotton output is less than the rate of growth per hectare yield, thus implying that acreage under cotton declined over the period.

[22] See Subramanian Swamy, *Price Structure in the People's Republic of China* (New Delhi, in press).

TABLE 9

RATES OF GROWTH OF VARIOUS NONFOODGRAIN CROPS, CHINA AND INDIA, 1952–56 to 1961–65
(% PER YEAR)

Crop	Production	Area	Yield per Hectare
India:			
Oilseeds	2.3	3.1	−0.8
Fibers	4.4	1.9	2.5
Others	3.0	−0.7	3.7
Total	2.9	1.2	1.7
China:			
Oilseeds	−4.2	−4.0	−0.2
Fibers	−1.3	−1.3	0.0
Others	0.0	1.2	−1.2
Total	−2.3	−1.8	−0.5

SOURCE.—Table A9.

irrigation, seeds—were probably denied to nonfoodgrain cultivation. Fertilizer, for example, was imported and paid for by rice exports at unfavorable prices. Hence imported fertilizer was probably used to raise the yield per hectare for rice. Shigeru Ishikawa has hypothesized that modernizing inputs were generally denied to agriculture and that this was one point of dispute between Chairman Mao and ex-President Liu Shao-ch'i.[23]

In India, the 2.9 percent rate of growth of nonfoodgrain crops is due to the relatively high rate of growth of fibers (4.4 percent). Further, this 4.4 percent reflects a 5.7 percent rate during the mid-1950s, when relative prices of fibers were rising. Oilseeds (excluding soybean), on the other hand, which accounted for over 25 percent of nonfoodgrain output, grew only 2.3 percent and thus limited the growth of total nonfoodgrain crops.

Yield per hectare for nonfoodgrain crops declined in China from 0.76 metric tons per hectare to 0.72, while in India it increased from 0.63 to 0.74. This result ties in with our earlier one that lands under foodgrain cultivation in China are inherently more fertile than in India. In fact, India, before Independence in 1947, followed a systematic policy of shifting the best lands to "cash" crop cultivation. After Independence, with worsening terms of trade facing foodgrain cultivation, there was no incentive to reverse this trend. This accounts in part for the more rapid growth of yield per hectare in India. The other factor is the proportion of land under irrigation. During the last 20 years, the greater proportion of new irrigated land was brought under "cash" crop cultivation in India, whereas in China it was under foodgrain cultivation.

[23] Shigeru Ishikawa, "Agrarian Reform and Its Productivity Effect—Implications of the Chinese Pattern," in *Structure and Development of Asian Economies* (Tokyo: Japan Economic Research Center, 1968).

Net Value-added in Agriculture, China and India, 1952–70

I have followed two procedures in estimating value-added in agriculture. The methodology for 1952–57 is based on the pioneering work of T. C. Liu and K. C. Yeh. There are, however, two principal differences in computational detail. First, the Liu-Yeh estimates of foodgrain and cotton output have been replaced by OSB estimates, and this accounts for almost the entire difference between my estimates and those of Liu-Yeh. Also, the figures used are for processed grain, that is, minus the husk. Table 10

TABLE 10

VALUE-ADDED IN AGRICULTURE, CHINA (BILLION YUAN; 1952 PRICES)

Item	1952	1953	1954	1955	1956	1957
Gross value of output:						
Plant products	22.98	23.40	23.82	26.21	26.85	27.96
Animal products	6.11	6.22	5.98	5.11	5.83	5.51
Forest products	1.19	1.49	1.73	1.68	1.69	2.04
Fishery products	0.63	0.72	0.87	0.96	1.00	1.18
Misc. products	2.18	2.22	2.26	2.29	2.35	2.36
Total	33.09	34.05	34.66	36.25	37.72	39.05
Deductible costs of production:						
Plant products (8% line 1)	1.84	1.87	1.91	2.10	2.15	2.24
Animal products	1.10	1.17	1.25	1.20	1.19	1.19
Forest products	0.04	0.04	0.05	0.05	0.05	0.06
Fishery products	0.03	0.04	0.04	0.05	0.05	0.06
Misc. products	0.24	0.25	0.25	0.25	0.26	0.26
Total	3.25	3.37	3.50	3.65	3.70	3.81
Gross value-added:						
Plant products	21.14	21.53	21.91	24.11	24.70	25.72
Animal products	5.01	5.04	4.73	3.91	4.64	4.32
Forest products	1.15	1.45	1.68	1.63	1.64	1.98
Fishery products	0.60	0.68	0.83	0.91	0.95	1.13
Misc. products	1.93	1.97	2.01	2.04	2.09	2.10
Total	29.83	30.67	31.16	32.60	34.02	35.25
Depreciation (2% line 18)	0.60	0.61	0.62	0.65	0.68	0.70
Net value-added (lines 18 − 19)	29.23	30.06	30.54	31.95	33.34	34.55

SOURCES.—Plant products from tables A7 and A8. All others from T. C. Liu and K. C. Yeh, *The Economy of the Chinese Mainland* (Princeton, N.J.: Princeton University Press, 1965). The price data are from Subramanian Swamy, *Price Structure in the People's Republic of China* (New Delhi, in press).

shows my estimates in some detail. All other data for 1952–57 are the Liu-Yeh estimates, accepted without change. Second, my final figures are in Indian prices derived from purchasing power calculation (see table 11).

The procedure for 1958–65 follows Liu's estimating technique, except that the official and official-based Chinese estimates were used for food-grains and raw cotton. Briefly, the Liu method projects the best linear-predictor relation between value-added in agriculture and total output of

TABLE 11

NET VALUE-ADDED IN AGRICULTURE, CHINA AND INDIA

	CHINA		INDIA	
YEAR	Net Value 1952 Prices (Billion Parity Rupees) (1)	Annual Change (%) (2)	Net Value 1948–49 Prices (Billion Parity Rupees) (3)	Annual Change (%) (4)
1952.........	58.46	...	44.4	...
1953.........	60.12	2.8	46.0	3.6
1954.........	61.08	1.6	49.8	8.3
1955.........	63.90	4.6	50.3	0.8
1956.........	66.68	4.3	50.2	0.0
1957.........	69.10	3.6	52.5	4.6
1958.........	78.40	13.4	50.1	−4.6
1959.........	72.46	−7.2	55.6	11.0
1960.........	59.00	−18.9	55.1	−0.9
1961.........	71.20	20.7	59.1	7.3
1962.........	73.86	3.7	59.1	0.0
1963.........	78.94	6.9	57.9	−2.0
1964.........	86.32	9.3	59.7	3.1
1965.........	87.24	0.1	65.1	9.0
1970.........	87.98	...	75.7	...

SOURCES.—Col. 1: 1952–57—See table 10. 1958–65—See text. 1970—Same technique as for 1958–65. Foodgrains (processed) output is taken as 192.0 MMT, Chou En-lai's claim. Fibers output is extrapolated at 12.2 percent per year, the 1965–68 rate claimed by Radio Peking on March 3, 1970. Col. 3: *Estimates of National Income and Product*, Conventional Series (New Delhi: Central Statistical Organization, 1971).

foodgrains and raw cotton. This technique works satisfactorily on Indian data; however, it is likely to lead to a slight overestimation of the Chinese rate of growth. Since Chinese plant products constitute about 70 percent of the total value-added in agriculture, foodgrains and raw cotton outputs should be a fairly satisfactory index of the value-added aggregate. But the coefficients of this predictor relation are based on the data for the 1952–57 period, when the nonplant agricultural products grew only 1.8 percent annually. In the projection of the value-added aggregate for 1958–65, this low rate is implicitly replaced by the plant rate of growth of 3.8 percent per year. Since there is sufficient reason to believe that livestock and fishery products did *not* grow as rapidly as plant products during 1958–65, the projected value-added figures may overestimate the rate of growth in China. With this cautionary remark, the value-added estimates for China and India may be interpreted.[24]

Although the rate of growth of foodgrain and nonfoodgrain crops was higher in India, the rate of growth of value-added in agriculture was a little *higher* in China (table 12). For the period 1952–65 the value-added

[24] Since Indian value-added aggregates have been analyzed elsewhere, the data validity tests are not presented here. The value-added estimates in table 11 are basically the official series (see Subramanian Swamy, "Economic Growth and Income Distribution in a Developing Nation: The Case of India" [G.R.D. diss., Harvard University, 1965]).

TABLE 12

RATE OF GROWTH OF VALUE-ADDED IN AGRICULTURE, CHINA AND INDIA (% PER YEAR)

Period	China	India
1952–56 to 1957–59	4.2	2.3
1957–59 to 1961–65	1.6	2.6
1952–56 to 1961–65	2.8	2.5
1961–65 to 1970	1.4	3.3
1952–56 to 1970	2.2	2.9

SOURCE.—Table 11.

aggregate's rate of growth was 2.8 percent in China and 2.5 percent in India.

It follows that the rate of growth of animal, forest, fishery, and other ancillary products was appreciably higher in China. This can be demonstrated simply. Since raw cotton (used as proxy for nonfood crops) comprises one-thirteenth of plant products in China, the rate of growth of plant products in China was (12 ÷ 13) (0.026) + (1 ÷ 13) (−0.013), or 2.40 percent. Also plant products comprise about 70 percent of the value-added in agriculture. Hence the rate of growth of value-added in agriculture in China was (0.7 × 0.024) + (0.3 × 0.038), or 2.82 percent, which checks with our earlier figure, 2.8 percent. For India, the estimate also checks: the rate of growth of plant products is (0.54 × 0.03) + (0.46 × 0.029), or 2.95 percent—higher than the Chinese rate. But the rate of growth of value-added in agriculture equals (0.73 × 0.0295) + (0.27 × 0.012), or 2.49 percent—lower than China's rate. Of course, the estimate of noncrop output which causes this shift in growth rates is the weakest component of the estimate for value-added in agriculture. The difficulty in obtaining livestock figures in India is well known; in China it must be even harder. There are certain unexplained absurdities in the Chinese livestock figures. Liu and Yeh, for example, notice that from 1956 to 1957 official figures of hog production show a 50 percent increase. Even after the correction by Liu-Yeh the hog figures seem to be overestimates.

If the time period is extended to 1970, the rate of growth of value-added in China drops to 2.2 percent. During 1963–70, the Chinese value-added aggregate grew only 1.4 percent, which is well below the 1954–63 trend rate of 2.8 percent per year. On the other hand, in India the rate of growth increased from 2.5 percent to 3.3 percent in 1963–70. Consequently the average annual rate of growth in China during 1952–70 is considerably lower than the corresponding Indian growth rate.

Appendix A
Tests of Validity of Chinese Grain Output Data

Any student of China faces a serious problem of choice. Which, if any, of the available estimates of foodgrains are to be accepted? Most China scholars seem to agree that the official Chinese figures are overestimates. But they disagree in every other respect. I, too, do not have all the facts at my command, although the estimates presented here—namely, the official Chinese *published* estimates (1952–57) and official Chinese *communicated* estimates (1952–65)—do not suffer, in my view, from the major drawback of the Sinologists' estimates: that the 1957 per capita grain production level was never again attained. Although this reason may not be analytically compelling, in choosing the *official published* cum *communicated* series, it is offered with the added note that *every major conclusion of this study would be only further strengthened if I were to use any other estimate.*

The OSB Grain Output Series for China

My estimates of grain production are presented in table 2. They do not basically contradict nor are they contradicted by the estimates of Sinologists for 1952–57 (although there are some differences of opinion on the underestimation involved in 1952). On the other hand, estimates for 1958–65 differ considerably from those of leading Sinologists. I therefore compare these statistics with other data.

Internal Consistency of Currently Available Estimates

R. M. Field has performed an interesting test of the validity of foodgrain output estimates. He makes two especially relevant observations. First, the difference between the *highest* estimate (Edwin Jones)[25] and the *lowest* estimate (J. R. Wenmohs)[26] is quite significant, especially if the change in output is broken down into that due to area and that due to yield per acre (table A3). Second, if we accept the 1957 output figure, then input data indicate a higher output figure for 1964.

Table A13 demonstrates the caution necessary in accepting Western estimates of foodgrains output. Table A14 shows four of the better-known Western estimates of China's foodgrain production, together with the "officially implied" series, the figures known popularly among Sinologists as "official" estimates, which were derived from various statements made by Chinese political leaders.

Several questions regarding the internal consistency of these figures may be raised:

First, if Chou En-lai's 1965 statement[27] that output for 1964 is "the best in the history" of China, then the 1964 estimate must exceed the previous best, namely, the 1958 estimate. While no Sinologist accepts the published 1958 estimate of 250 million metric tons, three of the four estimates are more than 200 million metric tons. If the 1958 figure did not fall below 205 million metric tons, then the various 1964 estimates in table A14 contradict Chou En-lai's statement.

Second, the estimates presented in table A14 are not supported by input data. In 1964, total chemical fertilizer used was 6.0 million metric tons,

[25] E. Jones, "Emerging Pattern of China's Economic Revolution," in *an Economic Profile of Mainland China* (Washington, D.C.: Joint Economic Committee, U.S. Congress, 1967).

[26] R. M. Field, "How Much Grain Does Communist China Produce?" (see n. 8 above).

[27] *Asahi Shimbun* (Tokyo), February 27, 1965. Earlier Chou had said that the 1961 output was worse than 1959 but better than 1957. This also contradicts all the estimates since, according to all four sources, 1961 is *worse* than 1957 (see L. Lichnowsky, "Agricultural Policy in Mainland China since 1949," *Monthly Bulletin of Agricultural Economics and Statistics*, UNFAO, Rome [October 1962]).

and acreage under food crops was 128.72 million hectares (see table A5 and A10). Assume now that the total increase in chemical fertilizer since 1957 (i.e., 6.0 MMT − 1.94 MMT, or 4.06 MMT) was distributed to food crops.[28] Assume, conservatively, that the marginal foodgrain product of fertilizer is 5 kilograms per kilogram of fertilizer,[29] and the average foodgrain yield per hectare is 1.50 million metric tons. Then the increase in foodgrains production from 1957 to 1964 should be at least $(5 \times 4.06) + (1.50 \times 7.83)$, or 32.05 million metric tons; and 1964 output should be at least $(185 + 32.05)$, or 217.05. In computing this figure, the yield-raising effects of capital inputs, modernization of agricultural organization, and the effect of new seeds have all been completely ignored. Nonetheless, the figure of 217 million metric tons is much larger than the Jones and "official" estimates.

Finally, the figures in table A14 seem unrealistic in per capita terms. No reliable estimate of population growth rate is available. However, judging by the statements of Chinese officials, the population growth rate probably did not fall below 2.0 percent during most of the period. In 1965, Chou En-lai told reporters in Cairo that the growth rate of population was about 2.5 percent per year. Premier Chou also told Edgar Snow that China hoped to *reduce* the rate to 2.0 percent by 1970, which implies that the rate then current was higher. The rate of population growth in China is assumed to be 2.2 percent on the average, the same as in India. Using this rate, we calculated per capita production figures (table A15).

According to all four estimates the 1958 or 1959 per capita production *was never again attained.* In fact, the Chinese seem to be falling further and further below this "peak." (This decrease would be unchanged even if net foodgrains imports were included.) It appears implausible that China *for over*

TABLE A1

NONFOODGRAIN AGRICULTURAL PRODUCTION, INDIA
(MMT)

Year	Fibers	Oilseeds	Others
1951–52	0.86	6.12	14.53
1952–53	0.86	5.85	16.07
1953–54	0.78	6.74	14.57
1954–55	0.81	5.88	15.10
1955–56	0.94	5.73	16.49
1956–57	1.05	6.36	17.58
1957–58	1.01	6.35	17.74
1958–59	1.16	7.30	16.97
1959–60	0.92	6.56	18.41
1960–61	1.06	6.98	20.17
1961–62	1.29	7.28	20.08
1962–63	1.25	7.39	19.28
1963–64	1.35	7.13	20.07
1964–65	1.33	8.56	21.33

SOURCES.—*Area, Production, and Yield of Principal Crops in India, 1949–50 to 1966–67* (New Delhi: Directorate of Economics and Statistics, Ministry of Food, Agriculture, Community Development and Cooperation, 1968).

NOTE.—The term "others" includes sugar cane, tobacco, vegetables, fruits, etc.

[28] For reasons, see R. M. Field, "How Much Grain Does Communist China Produce?" (see n. 8 above).

[29] For higher estimates, see Kao Kuang-chien, "Big Strides in China's Fertilizer Industry," *Jing Jih Daw Baw*, March 15, 1965, p. 15. T. C. Liu arrives at much lower marginal produce figures, but his estimate would be absurdly low for Indian land conditions, and I take it also to be unrealistic for China.

10 years has not been able to attain a previous peak. If this were true, such a major failure would probably have been reported through large-scale emigration via Hong Kong, as was done in 1960–61.

TABLE A2

ACREAGE UNDER NONFOODGRAINS, INDIA (MILLION HECTARES)

Year	Fibers	Oilseeds	Others	All Crops
1951–52	7.36	10.24	18.23	133.23
1952–53	7.09	11.53	16.76	137.68
1953–54	7.67	11.98	13.30	142.48
1954–55	8.23	10.07	17.39	144.09
1955–56	9.21	12.09	15.01	147.31
1956–57	9.28	12.49	16.22	149.49
1957–58	9.22	12.66	13.95	145.83
1958–59	9.29	13.00	14.03	151.62
1959–60	8.47	13.95	14.00	152.82
1960–61	8.70	13.77	14.15	152.72
1961–62	8.53	14.77	14.10	156.10
1962–63	9.27	15.34	15.66	156.77
1963–64	9.62	14.82	15.52	156.76
1964–65	9.66	15.26	16.08	159.10

SOURCE.—See table A1.

TABLE A3

NONFOODGRAIN AGRICULTURAL PRODUCTION, CHINA (MMT)

Year	Soybeans	Fibers	Oilseeds	Others
1952	9.52	1.49	3.74	7.01
1953	9.93	1.34	3.53	7.90
1954	9.08	1.26	3.87	8.46
1955	9.12	1.85	4.36	10.22
1956	10.23	1.75	4.60	10.45
1957	10.05	2.00	3.77	9.05
1958	10.50	2.10	4.24	n.a.
1959	11.50	2.41	n.a.	n.a.
1960	n.a.	n.a.	n.a.	n.a.
1961	5.50	1.10	2.30	5.93
1962	6.00	1.05	n.a.	n.a.
1963	6.50	1.22	n.a.	n.a.
1964	7.00	1.61	n.a.	n.a.
1965	7.50	1.85	3.40	11.70

SOURCES.—1952–58: Chen Nai-ruenn, *Chinese Economic Statistics* (Chicago: Aldine Publishing Co., 1966). 1959: My estimates. 1961–65: Soybeans (1961, 1965), oilseeds, and others—Edwin Jones, "Emerging Pattern of China's Economic Revolution," in *An Economic Profile of Mainland China* (Washington, D.C.: Joint Economic Committee, U.S. Congress, 1967). Fibers—E. Jones in *Mainland China in the World Economy* (U.S., Congress, House, Joint Economics Committee, 90th Cong., 1967), supplemented with my estimate of noncotton fibers.

TABLE A4

ACREAGE UNDER NONFOODGRAINS, CHINA
(MILLION HECTARES)

Year	Soybeans	Fibers	Oilseeds	Others	All Crops
1952.......	11.68	5.69	4.72	6.87	141.26
1953.......	12.36	5.28	4.53	7.67	144.04
1954.......	12.65	5.58	4.85	8.35	147.93
1955.......	11.44	5.94	5.66	9.64	151.08
1956.......	12.05	6.43	5.83	10.56	159.17
1957.......	12.75	5.95	5.89	11.75	157.24
1958.......	13.00	5.90	4.83	12.00	156.93
1959.......	n.a.	n.a.	n.a.	n.a.	n.a.
1960.......	n.a.	n.a.	n.a.	n.a.	n.a.
1961.......	7.00	4.0	3.50	7.70	140.9
1962.......	n.a.	n.a.	n.a.	n.a.	n.a.
1963.......	n.a.	n.a.	n.a.	n.a.	n.a.
1964.......	n.a.	n.a.	n.a.	n.a.	n.a.
1965.......	9.00	6.4	4.50	11.70	158.9

SOURCES.—1952–57: Chen Nai-ruenn, *Chinese Economic Statistics* (Chicago: Aldine Publishing Co., 1966). 1958: My estimate from various sources. 1961–65: Edwin Jones, "Emerging Pattern of China's Economic Revolution," *An Economic Profile of Mainland China* (Washington, D.C.: Joint Economic Committee, U.S. Congress, 1967). Also Edwin Jones in *Mainland China in the World Economy* (U.S., Congress, House, Joint Economics Committee, 90th Cong., 1967).

TABLE A5

SOWN ACREAGE UNDER FOODGRAINS, CHINA
(MILLION HECTARES)

Year	Rice	Wheat	Misc. Grain	Potatoes	Foodgrains
1952.......	28.4	24.8	50.5	8.7	112.3
1953.......	28.3	25.6	51.3	9.0	114.2
1954.......	28.7	27.0	50.9	9.8	116.3
1955.......	29.2	26.7	52.4	10.1	118.4
1956.......	35.5	27.3	52.7	11.0	124.3
1957.......	32.2	27.5	50.6	10.5	120.9
1958.......	32.7	26.6	45.7	16.3	121.2
1959.......	32.6	27.2	46.7	14.0	120.6
1960.......	31.1	27.5	46.6	13.4	118.7
1961.......	31.0	24.6	49.2	14.0	118.7
1962.......	33.1	25.7	53.3	14.4	126.5
1963.......	33.6	25.4	54.6	13.9	127.8
1964.......	33.8	25.0	55.9	13.5	128.7
1965.......	34.3	25.0	57.2	13.5	130.0

SOURCES.—1952–58: Chen Nai-ruenn, *Chinese Economic Statistics* (Chicago: Aldine Publishing Co., 1966). 1959–61: The percentage distribution from *Current Scene*, January 22, 1962, used to distribute the official figure for aggregate sown area under foodgrains. 1962–64: Estimated by me by the same method as for 1959–61. 1965: Percentage distribution from Edwin Jones, "Emerging Patterns of China's Economic Revolution," in *An Economic Profile of Mainland China* (Washington, D.C.: Joint Economic Committee, U.S. Congress, 1967). Area estimate is by the author.

TABLE A6

Sown Acreage under Foodgrains, India
(Million Hectares)

Year	Rice	Wheat	Misc. Grain	Potatoes	Foodgrains
1951–52....	29.8	9.5	57.7	0.4	97.4
1952–53....	30.0	9.8	62.3	0.4	102.5
1953–54....	31.3	10.7	67.1	0.4	109.5
1954–55....	30.8	11.3	65.8	0.5	108.4
1955–56....	31.5	12.4	66.7	0.4	111.0
1956–57....	32.3	13.5	63.3	0.4	109.5
1957–58....	32.3	11.7	65.5	0.5	110.0
1958–59....	33.2	12.6	68.9	0.6	115.3
1959–60....	33.8	13.4	68.6	0.6	116.4
1960–61....	34.1	12.9	68.6	0.5	116.1
1961–62....	34.7	13.6	68.9	0.5	117.7
1962–63....	34.9	13.7	67.4	0.5	116.5
1963–34....	35.6	13.5	67.2	0.5	116.8
1964–65....	36.4	13.5	67.6	0.6	118.1

Source.—*Area, Production, and Yield of Principal Crops in India, 1949–50 to 1966–67* (New Delhi: Directorate of Economics and Statistics, Ministry of Food, Agriculture, Community Development and Cooperation, 1968).

TABLE A7

Processed Output of Foodgrains, China

	MMT				%			
Year	Rice	Wheat	Misc. Grain	Grain Equiv. Potatoes	Rice	Wheat	Misc. Grain	Potatoes
1952...	49.3	15.4	47.4	15.1	38.8	12.1	37.3	11.9
1953...	51.3	15.6	46.6	15.4	39.8	12.1	36.2	11.9
1954...	51.0	19.9	45.4	15.6	38.7	15.1	34.4	11.8
1955...	56.2	19.6	50.6	17.4	39.1	13.6	35.2	12.1
1956...	59.4	21.1	49.1	20.1	39.7	14.1	32.8	13.4
1957...	62.5	20.1	48.5	20.1	41.3	13.3	32.1	13.3
1958...	68.9	20.7	47.7	35.0	40.0	12.0	27.7	20.3
1959...	65.5	23.0	53.5	17.3	41.1	14.4	33.6	10.9
1960...	56.2	18.9	35.1	19.9	43.2	14.5	27.0	15.3
1961...	57.6	21.3	61.4	16.8	36.7	13.6	39.1	10.7
1962...	62.4	21.0	60.5	19.2	38.3	12.9	37.1	11.8
1963...	69.9	21.2	61.5	22.6	39.9	12.1	35.1	12.9
1964...	78.9	21.7	63.0	26.6	41.5	11.4	33.1	14.0
1965...	82.9	20.4	59.7	29.0	43.2	10.6	31.1	16.1

Sources.—1952–57: Chen Nai-Ruenn, *Chinese Economic Statistics* (Chicago: Aldine Publishing Co., 1966). 1958: The output, 215 MMT, distributed by the official published distribution. 1959: L. Lichnowsky, "Agricultural Policy in Mainland China since 1949," *Monthly Bulletin of Agricultural Economics and Statistics*, UNFAO, Rome (October 1962). 1960: Distribution of total output according to *Current Scene*, January 22, 1962; *Neue Zuercher Zeitung*, January 30–31, 1962, JPRS no. 13052. 1961: Lichnowsky, corrected table 1; and *Neue Zuercher Zeitung*, p. 1. 1962–64: Total output of grains is distributed by the *Current Scene's* percentage distribution. 1965: Edwin Jones, "Emerging Pattern of China's Economic Revolution," in *An Economic Profile of Mainland China* (Washington, D.C.: Joint Economic Committee, U.S. Congress, 1967).

Notes.—Miscellaneous grain includes millet, corn, *kaoliang* [sorghus vulgare], barley, buckwheat oats, and press millet, small bean, green bean, broad bean, peas, etc. Processing ratios are also from *Current Scene*.

TABLE A8

OUTPUT OF FOODGRAINS, INDIA

Year	MMT				%			
	Rice	Wheat	Misc. Grain	Grain Equiv. Potatoes	Rice	Wheat	Misc. Grain	Potatoes
1951–52	21.3	6.2	24.5	0.7	40.4	11.8	46.5	1.3
1952–53	22.3	7.5	29.4	0.7	38.2	12.5	49.1	1.2
1953–54	28.2	8.0	33.6	0.8	39.9	11.3	47.6	1.1
1954–55	25.2	9.0	33.8	0.8	36.6	13.1	49.1	1.2
1955–56	27.6	8.8	30.5	0.8	41.8	13.0	45.1	1.2
1956–57	29.0	9.4	31.5	0.7	41.1	13.3	44.6	1.0
1957–58	25.5	8.0	30.8	0.8	39.2	12.3	47.3	1.2
1958–59	30.8	10.0	36.3	0.9	39.5	12.8	46.5	1.2
1959–60	31.7	10.3	34.7	1.0	41.8	13.3	44.7	1.3
1960–61	34.6	11.0	36.4	1.0	42.7	13.3	43.9	1.2
1961–62	35.7	12.1	34.9	0.8	43.8	14.5	41.8	1.0
1962–63	32.0	10.8	35.7	1.1	40.2	13.6	44.9	1.4
1963–64	36.9	9.9	33.4	0.9	46.5	12.2	41.2	1.1
1964–65	39.0	12.3	37.7	1.3	43.2	13.6	41.7	1.4

SOURCES.—*Bulletin on Food Statistics* (New Delhi: Directorate of Economics and Statistics, Ministry of Food, Agriculture, Community Development and Cooperation, 1972); and *Basic Statistics relating to the Indian Economy* (New Delhi: Planning Commission, 1969).

NOTES.—Miscellaneous grain includes *jowar* [great millet], *bajra* [bulrush millet], maize, *ragi* [finger millet], small millets, *gran*, *tur* [pigeon pea], barley, and other pulses. Grain-equivalent potatoes are sweet and Irish potatoes converted to grain-equivalence by multiplying by 0.25.

TABLE A9

LEVEL AND RATE OF GROWTH OF NONFOODGRAIN CROP, CHINA AND INDIA

Period	Fibers		Oilseeds		Others		Total	
	China	India	China	India	China	India	China	India
	Absolute Level Production (MMT)							
1952–56	1.54	0.85	13.60	6.06	8.81	15.35	23.95	22.26
1957–59	2.17	1.07	14.60	6.67	9.05	17.43	25.82	25.17
1961–65	1.37	1.26	9.35	7.47	8.82	20.18	19.54	28.91
	Area (Million Hectares)							
1952–56	5.78	7.91	17.15	11.18	8.66	16.14	31.59	35.23
1957–59	5.93	9.26	18.24	12.72	11.88	14.73	36.05	36.71
1961–65	5.20	9.36	12.00	14.79	9.70	15.10	26.90	39.25
	Production Rate of Growth (% per Year)							
1952–56 to 1961–65	−1.3	4.4	−4.2	2.3	0.0	3.0	−2.3	2.9
1952–56 to 1957–59	8.6	5.7	1.8	2.4	0.7	3.2	1.9	3.1
1957–59 to 1961–65	−9.2	3.3	−8.9	2.2	−0.5	3.0	−5.6	2.8
	Area Rate of Growth (% per Year)							
1952–56 to 1961–65	−1.3	1.9	−4.0	3.1	1.2	−0.7	−1.8	1.2
1952–56 to 1957–59	0.8	3.9	1.5	3.2	7.9	−2.3	3.3	1.0
1957–59 to 1961–65	−2.6	0.2	−8.4	3.0	−4.0	0.5	−5.6	1.3

SOURCES.—Tables A1 through A4.

TABLE A10

INPUT IN CHINESE AGRICULTURE

Year	Sown Area (Million Hectares) (1)	Total Fertilizer Use (MMT) (2)	Total H.P. (Millions) (3)	Multiple Cropping Index (4)
1952	112.30	0.32	0.031	134.00
1953	114.20	0.59	0.042	135.30
1954	116.34	0.80	0.079	136.70
1955	118.40	1.26	0.125	138.00
1956	124.29	1.61	0.300	139.40
1957	120.89	1.94	0.560	140.60
1958	121.20	2.72	0.690	142.00
1959	120.60	2.93	0.898	140.60
1960	118.72	3.67	1.221	130.00
1961	118.66	3.54	2.230	133.00
1962	126.49	4.22	3.600	136.30
1963	127.81	5.11	5.200	140.00
1964	128.72	6.00	7.000	143.10
Average:				
1952–56	117.1	0.90	0.115	136.75
1957–59	120.8	2.50	0.715	141.10
1961–64	126.3	4.70	4.508	138.51

SOURCES.—Col. 1: Col. 4 × cultivated acreage ÷ 100. Cultivated acreage from Subramanian Swamy and Shahid J. Burke, "Foodgrains Output in the People's Republic of China," *China Quarterly*, no. 41 (January-March 1970). Col. 2: 1952–53—M. R. Larsen, "China's Agriculture under Communism," in *An Economic Profile of Mainland China* (Washington, D.C.: Joint Economic Committee, U.S. Congress, 1967). 1954–64—from Swamy and Burki. Col. 3: 1952–56—Estimated from data in Fukushima Yutaka, "Japanese Analysis on Communes and Agricultural Mechanization in Communist China," *Chugoku Shiryo Geppo*, no. 144, March 28, 1960, pp. 1–35. 1957–64—Shahid J. Burki, *A Study of Chinese Communes*, East Asia Monographs (Cambridge, Mass.: Harvard University Press, 1969). Col. 4: Subramanian Swamy, *Economic Policy in China and India*, forthcoming; Shigeru Ishikawa, "Factors Affecting China's Agriculture in the Coming Decade," working paper, Investigation and Research no. 42–28, Institute of Asian Economic Affairs, Tokyo, also Anthony Tang, "Policy and Performance in Agriculture," in *Economic Trends in Communist China*, ed. Alexander Eckstein, Walter Galenson, and T. C. Liu (Chicago: Aldine Publishing Co., 1968).

NOTES.—Total fertilizer includes imports and domestic production of N, P_2O_5, and K_2O. Total horsepower includes all pumps, electric or oil generated, and tractors.

TABLE A11

INPUT IN INDIAN AGRICULTURE

Year	Sown Area (Million Hectares) (1)	Total Fertilizer Use (MMT) (2)	Total H.P. (Millions) (3)	Multiple Cropping Index (4)
1951–52........	97.0	0.073	0.598	111.59
1952–53........	102.1	0.108	0.704	111.53
1953–54........	109.1	0.094	0.810	112.36
1954–55........	107.9	0.113	0.916	112.70
1955–56........	110.6	0.152	1.022	114.06
1956–57........	111.1	0.168	1.128	114.25
1957–58........	109.5	0.230	1.383	112.98
1958–59........	114.8	0.231	1.635	115.01
1959–60........	115.8	0.324	1.887	114.96
1960–61........	115.6	0.363	2.136	114.69
1961–62........	117.2	0.394	2.388	115.33
1962–63........	116.0	0.564	2.640	115.09
1963–64........	116.3	0.601	2.892	115.07
1964–65........	117.5	0.710	3.144	115.33
Average:				
1952–56....	105.8	0.100	0.810	112.40
1957–59....	112.2	0.200	1.381	114.20
1961–65....	117.0	0.500	2.640	115.08

SOURCES.—Col. 1: Col. 4 × cultivated area ÷ 100. Cultivated area from *Basic Statistics relating to the Indian Economy* (New Delhi: Planning Commission, 1966). Col. 2: *Fertilizer Statistics* (New Delhi: Fertilizer Association of India, 1966–67. Col. 3: 1951, 1956, 1961—*Handbook of Agriculture* (New Delhi: Indian Council of Agricultural Research, 1967). Figures for other years are interpolated and extrapolated. Col. 4: *Basic Statistics relating to the Indian Economy.*

TABLE A12

RATE OF GROWTH OF FOOD CROPS, CHINA AND INDIA (% PER YEAR)

PERIOD	RICE		WHEAT		MISC. GRAINS		POTATOES	
	China	India	China	India	China	India	China	India
1952–56 to 1957–59:								
Q...........	5.1	3.3	3.8	3.7	1.1	1.9	9.2	3.0
A...........	2.0	1.5	0.8	4.1	−2.0	0.8	12.4	5.6
Q/A	3.1	1.8	3.0	−0.4	3.1	1.1	−3.2	−2.6
1957–59 to 1961–65:								
Q...........	1.4	4.5	−0.2	4.2	4.1	1.5	−1.1	2.1
A...........	0.4	1.5	−1.5	1.2	2.5	0.6	0.4	0.0
Q/A	1.0	3.0	1.3	3.0	1.6	0.9	−1.5	2.1
1952–56 to 1961–65:								
Q...........	3.1	4.0	1.6	3.9	2.7	1.7	3.5	2.5
A...........	1.1	1.5	−0.5	2.5	0.5	0.7	5.6	2.5
Q/A	2.0	2.5	2.1	1.4	2.2	1.0	−2.1	0.0

SOURCE.—Table 6.
NOTE.—Q = output, A = area, Q/A = yield per hectare.

TABLE A13

SOURCES OF INCREASED FOODGRAINS OUTPUT, 1957–65
(%)

Source	Wenmohs	Jones
Area	−0.2	+6.4
Yield per hectare	−4.8	+8.6
Total change in output	−5.0	+15.0

SOURCE.—R. M. Field, "How Much Grain Does Communist China Produce?" *China Quarterly*, no. 33 (January-March 1968).

TABLE A14

VARIOUS ESTIMATES OF PRODUCTION OF GRAIN IN CHINA
(MMT)

Year	Wenmohs (1)	Klatt (2)	Dawson (3)	Jones (4)	Official (5)
1957	185	185	185	185	n.a.
1958	194	205	205	250	250
1959	168	190	170	270	n.a.
1960	160	160	160	150	150
1961	167	165	170	162	160
1962	178	180	180	174	174
1963	179	175	185	183	184
1964	185	190	195	200	300
1965	180	185	193	200	200
1966	170	180	190	200–210	150–210
1967	n.a.	190	n.a.	n.a.	159–221
1968	n.a.	n.a.	n.a.	n.a.	n.a.

SOURCES.—Cols. 1 and 3: R. M. Field, "How Much Grain Does Communist China Produce?" *China Quarterly*, no. 33 (January-March 1968). Col. 2: Werner Klatt, "Grain Production—Comment," *China Quarterly*, no. 35 (July-September 1968). Col. 4: Edwin Jones, "Emerging Pattern of China's Economic Revolution," in *An Economic Profile of Mainland China* (Washington, D.C.: Joint Economic Committee, U.S. Congress, 1967). Col. 5: 1960 and 1961—Mao told Viscount Montgomery, Sunday *Times* (London), October 15, 1961, that 1960 output had been 150 MMT, and the preliminary estimate for 1961 was 160 MMT. 1962—Chou En-lai, *Dawn* (Pakistan), April 11, 1963, said that 1962 output was better than 1961, and 1961 was better than 1960. Further, the 1962 increase over 1960 was about 24 MMT. Using Mao's figure for 1961, I put the 1962 figure at 174 MMT. 1963—Chou En-lai told Edgar Snow, *Ashai Shimbun* (Tokyo), February 27, 1965, that the 1964 output was about 200 MMT. 1965—*Chinese News*, Summary, April 28, 1966, p. 1; also see Field. 1966 and 1967—See source in *Current Scene* (January 1968).

TABLE A15

ESTIMATED PER CAPITA PRODUCTION ACCORDING TO SINOLOGISTS
(KG PER HEAD PER YEAR)

Year	Wenmohs (1)	Klatt (2)	Dawson (3)	Jones (4)
1957	233.3	233.3	233.3	233.3
1958	239.4	253.0	253.0	308.5
1959	202.9	229.4	211.3	326.0
1960	189.1	189.1	189.1	177.3
1961	193.1	190.8	196.6	187.3
1962	201.4	203.6	203.6	196.9
1963	198.1	193.7	204.8	202.6
1964	200.4	205.8	211.2	216.6
1965	190.8	196.1	204.6	212.0
1966	176.2	186.7	197.0	207.4–217.8
1967	n.a.	192.8	n.a.	n.a.

SOURCE.—Table A14 and col. 4 of table 2. The grain figures are deflated by 20 percent to arrive at the processed figures.

III. Industrial Production

Introduction

Modern factory establishments have received a great deal of attention in China and India. It was clear to both countries well before the 1940s that the network of factory establishments, or industries, was essential for sustained economic growth, political independence, and world power. It is therefore no surprise that both countries have spent a sizable proportion of their resources on modern industries. Industrialization was the central focus of planning, and when the two countries established Planning Commissions (India in 1950 and China in 1952), the documents put out by the commissions left no doubt about the emphasis of planning:

> The key link in the development of the national economy during the transition period is the development of heavy industry, because only through the development of heavy industry is it possible to realize the socialist industrialization of the country, to develop the national economy of the country as a whole, and to provide for the transformation of the economy of the country on the basis of socialist principles.[30]
>
> While agriculture and industry must be regarded as closely linked parts of the same process of development, there is no doubt that industry has a leading role in securing rapid economic advance. Industrial development, and especially the development of basic and heavy industries, must be regarded as a part of a comprehensive design of development which ultimately links the industrial and rural economy, the economy of large-scale and of small-scale units, and the economy of the major industrial centers as well as of the smaller towns and villages, bringing them into a closed relationship with one another, thus assuming a high degree of mobility and economic integration within the economy as a whole.[31]

In this chapter we examine the performance of industry in some detail.

Index of Industrial Production, Official Series, 1951–70

To facilitate exposition, conclusions based on an acceptance of official series of both countries are first considered (table 13). The rate of growth

[30] Tzeng Wen-ching, *Socialist Industrialization of China*, JPRS no. 3800 (Moscow, 1959), chap. 3.

[31] *Third Five-Year Plan* (New Delhi: Planning Commission, 1961), pp. 24–25.

of industrial production on the basis of uncorrected official figures is quite high in China compared with India. The index for China rose from 100 in 1951 to 626 in 1965 and to 802 in 1970. For India the index rose from 100 to 251 and to 320 over the same years. If the base year is shifted to 1956, the difference between Chinese and Indian industrial performance *narrows* considerably. The Chinese index increased from 100 in 1956 to 301 in 1970; that for India from 100 to 242. It follows, even by Chinese official claims, that the Chinese rate of growth of industrial production decelerated over the period 1951–70, and in some periods, for example, 1960–63, the negative rates were quite substantial. In India, on the other hand, industrial production accelerated significantly during the later years.

TABLE 13

INDEX OF INDUSTRIAL PRODUCTION, OFFICIAL SERIES, CHINA AND INDIA

	CHINA		INDIA	
YEAR	1951=100	1956=100	1951=100	1956=100
1951.........	100.0	37.8	100.0	73.5
1952.........	130.1	48.8	103.1	75.8
1953.........	169.3	63.5	105.9	77.9
1954.........	197.1	73.9	113.1	83.2
1955.........	208.0	78.0	125.0	91.9
1956.........	266.7	100.0	136.0	100.0
1957.........	291.1	111.4	141.8	104.3
1958.........	493.9	185.2	146.5	107.7
1959.........	687.7	257.9	159.0	116.9
1960.........	887.5	332.8	117.0	130.1
1961.........	n.a.	n.a.	188.2	138.4
1962.........	n.a.	n.a.	204.8	150.6
1963.........	490.7	184.0	221.5	162.9
1964.........	564.3	211.6	237.7	174.8
1965.........	625.6	234.6	250.9	184.5
1966.........	751.7	281.8	269.7	198.3
1967.........	n.a.	n.a.	268.0	197.0
1968.........	689.3	258.5	285.7	209.6
1969.........	n.a.	n.a.	306.2	225.1
1970.........	802.2	300.8	320.3	242.0

SOURCES.—China: 1951–59—Chen Nai-ruenn, *Chinese Economic Statistics* (Chicago: Aldine Publishing Co., 1966). 1960–65—Official sources cited in R. M. Field, "Chinese Communist Industrial Production," in *An Economic Profile of Mainland China* (Washington, D.C.: Joint Economic Committee, U.S. Congress, 1967), p. 273. 1966 and 1968—Official sources cited in R. M. Field, "Industrial Production in Communist China," *China Quarterly*, no. 43 (July-September 1970). 1970—Chou En-lai as reported by Edgar Snow in *Epoca*, February 28, 1971. India: *Basic Statistics relating to the Indian Economy* (New Delhi: Planning Commission, 1969), and *Economic Survey, 1970–71* (New Delhi: Ministry of Finance, 1971).

I now inquire into the reliability of these indexes, to see whether these findings can be sustained on the basis of more reliable data. Since figures for 1959–65 are not available in significant detail for China, a comparison with India is quite difficult. This, of course, is not the only difficulty. The index numbers in both countries reflect biases in scope, valuation, and comparability over time. Space is therefore devoted here to a systematic examination of these problems before considering the conclusions. The Chinese index is first examined.[32]

Biases of Scope, China

Industry is defined in China as "the materially productive sector of extracting and collecting natural material wealth in whose creation no human efforts are involved, and of processing such wealth and agricultural products."[33] That is, industry is comprised of three sectors: (1) extracting, (2) collecting, and (3) processing. This definition includes portions of agriculture and services which are normally classified under industry (especially since 1958), and so is freight transport if it is provided by the factory.

Second, industry also includes handicrafts, in particular, the "handicraft factories." These factories are distinguished from the "individual handicrafts" in that the latter hires three or fewer workers and apprentices. If the factory has four or more employees, it is considered a small-scale enterprise, unless (1) it has thirty-one or more employees, or (2) it has sixteen or more employees and mechanical power, or (3) it is an independent electric power plant with capacity over 15 kilowatts. In such cases it is classified as a large-scale enterprise. By these definitions, twenty-one major groups with 250 branches are recognized.

Third, the indices in table 13 are for gross value of output. The Chinese derive the gross value of output by the *gong chaang faa*, or the "factory method," a concept which measures output in current ex-factory prices after elimination of intraenterprise turnover. Specifically, it consists of the following: (1) the value of the finished output produced during a given period, including raw materials, basic, and supplementary materials used in production; (2) the value of semi-finished products sold during the given period; (3) the value of changes in stock of semi-finished products and goods in process during the given period; and (4) the value of the work of an industrial nature completed during the given period, including major repairs to the machinery and equipment of the enterprise done by its own production workers.[34]

Obviously, the *only item outside the scope* of industrial production is the intraenterprise turnover, that is, semi-finished products produced for further fabrication *within* the enterprise.

Fourth, this factory method leads to significant double counting, which increases with the complexity of production. Increasing number of stages of production means more double counting; which imparts an upward bias to the index over time. Significant multiple counting is a fact; and according to a Chinese student it accounted for 61.8 percent of

[32] See also Chao Kang, *The Rate and Pattern of Industrial Growth in Communist China* (Ann Arbor: University of Michigan Press, 1965); and T. C. Liu and K. C. Yeh (see n. 1 above).

[33] *Industrial Statistics* (Wuhan: Hwubeei Dah Shyue 1960), p. 7.

[34] Chen Nai-ruenn, *Chinese Economic Statistics* (Chicago: Aldine Publishing Co., 1966), p. 37.

the gross value of industrial output in 1954.[35] Furthermore, the extent of double counting, by this method, varies inversely with the degree of vertical integration. Thus industrial output was somewhat reduced in 1956[36] when socialist collectivization was intensified, and exaggerated in 1958 when decentralization was implemented. This bias is especially serious in output statistics of iron ore, coke, steel ingots, other steel, nonferrous metal ores, pulp and paper, petroleum products, which account for nearly 30 percent of the output in the index.

Fifth, enterprises have been known to include in output sales to other enterprises without the slightest change in the product. For instance, in order to meet their production quotas, two textile firms may exchange raw materials with nominal processing. Under the factory method this exchange shows up twice.[37]

Sixth, although it is explicitly stated that some products be excluded, they are often included. For instance, chemical fertilizer output includes granular and bacterial fertilizer; chemical insecticides include vegetable insecticides made by crude methods.[38]

Seventh, profits of enterprises are calculated as a percentage of cost. There is thus a tendency to run down fixed assets and inflate costs.

Finally, in the early years firms underreported to evade taxes. In later years these firms were absorbed by socialization, and the rise in output thereafter is therefore partly illusory.

The biases noted above influence the value of industrial production in a variety of ways. However, the effects may be divided into two groups: (1) those on aggregate production, and (2) those on its rate of growth. Since eight biases tend to enlarge the scope of production—for example, to include nonindustrial outputs and already used-up intermediate products—they would inflate the aggregate value. They would also lend an upward bias to the rate of growth of industrial production. Further, with economic growth, the effect of these biases becomes increasingly serious. It may be concluded that the consideration of scope alone necessitates a reworking of the estimates.

Biases of Valuation, China

The index of industrial production is derived simply as the Laspreyres index, that is, conversion of the gross value series into an index. The

[35] "Several Problems of Computing the Gross Value of Industrial Output," *Toong Jih Gong Tzuoh Tong Shiun*, no. 17 (1956), pp. 1–4. There may have been an error in the original article, since 61.8 percent seems incredible. Or perhaps the author calculated the ratio of gross value-added to gross value. The latter ratio is about 35 percent, which means the cost and intermediate products are 65 percent of gross value of industrial output.

[36] "Diverse Opinions on the Methods of Computing the Gross Value of Industrial Output," *Toong Jih Gong Tzuoh Tong Shiun*, no. 24 (1956), pp. 5–10.

[37] "Gross Value and Net Value of Output," *Toong Jih Gong Tzuoh*, no. 2 (1958), p. 28.

[38] "Problems of Gross Value of Output in Chemical Industry," *Huah Shyua Gong Yeh*, no. 15 (1959), pp. 35–36.

common practice, followed in India, is to use value-added as the weights and *not* base year prices. These weights raise several questions about the index of industrial production; and their relevance for the Chinese index is now considered. During 1952 prices of producer goods in China were very high due to the demands of the Korean war. Also, more important, the relative (to consumer goods) price structure was heavily in favor of producer goods because of the depressed price level of consumer goods. This depressed price level was the direct result of the *San Faan* and *Wuu Faan* movements. Thus, use of the Laspeyres index assigns a very high weight to a fast-growing sector, that is, producer goods, and a relatively low weight to a slow-growing sector, namely, consumer goods.

Even if value-added figures were used as weights, the problems remain because the value-added shares are themselves dependent on the price structure. One reason is that the producer goods' prices were much higher in 1952 than in later years (as table 14 shows), and this would bias upward the value-added shares in 1952 prices.

TABLE 14

PRICES FOR SELECTED MACHINERY PRODUCTS, CHINA (YUAN PER UNIT)

Item	1952	1956
Sewing machine	190.0	108.6
8-inch water pumps	1590.0	424.0
Tip cart	6583.7	6400.0
Sprayer	28.4	20.0
Threshing machine	90.3	66.0
51-type ploy	25.0	15.8

SOURCES.—Lo Chin-hua, "A Problem of Using the Gross Value to Check the Production Plan in the Local Machinery Industries," *Toong Jih Gong Tzuoh*, no. 4 (1957), p. 6. (The source cited in Chao Kang, *The Rate and Pattern of Industrial Growth in Communist China* [Ann Arbor: University of Michigan Press, 1965], p. 20.) I assume Lo Chin-hua is referring to 1956 when he says "recent price."

The second reason is that new products are priced in China on the basis of test manufacturing expenses with a markup of about 15 percent for research expenses, which makes for very high initial prices. For example, according to Fan Ro-yi, a Chinese economist, a 6,000-kilowatt engine for steamships, introduced in 1955, was priced at 1,320,000 yuan.[39] In 1956, by the usual rules of price formation, its price was at 380,000 yuan only 33 percent of the price the previous year! This means that since new products tend to grow fast, the high price weight produces an upward bias in the rate of growth.

Thus, valuation procedures, like scope, lend an upward bias to the rate of growth of industrial production in China.

Biases in Comparability, China

There are also the problems of comparability over time. For instance, aquatic products and timber were shifted from agriculture to industry in

[39] Fan Ro-yi, "More on the Price Policy for Heavy Industry Products," *Jing Jih Yan Jiou*, no. 3 (1957).

1956. Also in 1956, when socialization was completed, a good portion of handicrafts output was classified under industrial production. In 1958 with the Great Leap Forward the classification of production became even more unclear.

We can conclude that the index of industrial production needs to be recomputed not only because of the upward bias in the rate of growth but also because the divergence between theoretically desirable criteria of scope, valuation, and comparability, and Chinese official practice is too wide.

Biases of Scope, Valuation, and Comparability, India

The Central Statistics Organization (CSO) publishes an index of industrial production. However, during the last 20 years its scope, valuation, and comparability have changed. The first index, with a base year of 1946, included thirty-five items and was a linear arithmetic average with value-added in the base year as weights. In 1956 a new index with 1951 as base was introduced. It included eighty-eight items; and the earlier thirty-five items accounted for 75 percent of the value-added for eighty-eight items. In 1962 the base was shifted to 1956 with 201 items, and the former eighty-eight items accounted for 78 percent of the value-added for the 201 items. In late 1968 this base was shifted to 1960, and the new list includes 449 items. Because of all these changes a choice has to be made—first, concerning the base to be used for comparison with China; and second, concerning the set of items to be taken as fixed. Furthermore, some scope changes were made within the industrial category; for example, in the 1960 base series, grinding wheels were transferred from the subsector "machinery except electrical machinery" to "nonmetallic mineral products except petroleum and coal products"; but these changes are minor. Table 15 gives detailed information regarding scope and weights used in the index of industrial production in India.

Even with the expansion from eighty-eight to 449 items, total value-added for the eighty-eight items in 1960 is over 75 percent of that of the 449 items. Obviously, additional 361 items did not play a dominant role in the weight structure. Some of the scope expansion came about purely by dividing major categories up to fifty-three subcategories. Thus, in the 1956 classification, the number of 1951 items is not eighty-eight but 122.

Although no serious problem is posed by the expansion of items under the scope of industrial production, the items covered in the expanded scope exclude many industrial items for which statistics are collected. For example, the *Monthly Statistics of Production of Selected Industries*, published by the Central Statistical Organization, contains over 150 items not included in the industrial production index. Other governmental agencies, such as the Directorate General of Technical Development, publish in their annual reports a variety of statistics of industrial output and capacity not published elsewhere. The accompanying statement lists

TABLE 15

INDEX NUMBERS OF INDUSTRIAL PRODUCTION, ITEM COVERAGE AND WEIGHTS ALLOTTED, INDIA

Division	Industry Group	1951 = 100 No. Items	1951 = 100 Weights (%)	1956 = 100 No. Items	1956 = 100 Weights (%)	1960 = 100 No. Items	1960 = 100 Weights (%)
1.......	Mining and quarrying	2	7.16	2	7.47	35	9.72
2, 3.....	Manufacturing	...	...	198	88.85	413	84.91
5.......	Electricity	1	2.16	1	3.68	1	5.37
20, 21...	Food	5	11.85	8	19.99	15	12.09
22......	Beverage and tobacco	1	1.50	1	1.49	2	2.22
23......	Textiles	12	48.01	19	41.76	20	27.06
24......	Footwear, other wearing apparel, and made-up textile goods	1	0.85	2	0.28	3	0.21
25......	Wood and cork except furniture	1	0.21	4	0.24	6	0.80
26......	Furniture and fixtures	0	0.00	0	0.00	1	0.39
27......	Paper products	1	1.57	4	1.39	6	1.61
29......	Leather and fur products except footwear and other wearing apparel	1	0.27	3	0.18	5	0.43
30......	Rubber products	5	3.35	24	3.04	26	2.22
31......	Chemicals and chemical products	15	4.16	45	3.58	138	7.26
32......	Products of petroleum and coal	0	0.00	1	3.79	9	1.45
33......	Nonmetallic mineral products except products of petroleum and coal	13	3.33	14	2.47	16	3.85
34......	Basic metal industries	6	8.84	23	9.25	27	7.38
35......	Metal products except machinery and transport equipment	5	2.57	13	0.99	18	2.51
36......	Machinery except electrical machinery	6	0.59	15	1.10	71	3.38
37......	Electrical machinery, apparatus, appliances, and supplies	11	1.46	14	2.41	21	3.05
38......	Transport equipment	2	2.92	7	2.86	15	7.77
39......	Miscellaneous	0	0.00	1	0.03	14	1.23
Total .	...	88	100.00	201	100.00	449	100.00

SOURCE.—1951: S. L. Shetty, "Index Numbers of Industrial Production," *Economic and Political Weekly*, no. 17 (1969). 1956–60: *Reserve Bank of India Bulletin* (Bombay) (August 1968), p. 1018.

some products for which data are available but which are excluded from the index.

Obviously, there are problems of scope and comparability in the Indian index of industrial production. Some of them arise because, with economic growth, the number of industrial items produced expands rapidly. There is little one can do statistically except to constantly revise the index. Obviously there is a limit to the frequency of revision; in this study I have adopted the scope of industrial production followed in 1956 (see table 16).

TABLE 16

INDUSTRIAL ITEMS OUTSIDE THE SCOPE OF THE INDEX OF INDUSTRIAL PRODUCTION, INDIA, 1956

Industry Group	Items excluded from Index
Metal mining	Two ferrous and eight nonferrous products
Nonmetallic minerals	Fifteen items such as china clay, limestone, mica, steatite, etc.
Textiles	Leather cloth, linoleum, tyrecord, etc.
Paper and paper products	Hardboard, insulation board
Rubber products	Industrial belts, camel black, etc.
Heavy organic chemicals	Five items such as acetic acid, ethyl, acetate, yeast, etc.
Heavy inorganic chemicals	Sixteen items such as potassium chlorate, chlorate, bromide, chromic acid, nitrous oxide, etc.
Synthetic resins and plastics	Polystyrene, PVC, polythene, etc.
Fertilizers	Ammonium chloride, etc.
Paints	Red lead and N lacquers
Pharmaceuticals	Large variety of items including penicillin, vitamins, sulpha drugs, etc.
Synthetic fibers	Nylon
Toilet preparations	Tooth paste and tooth powder
Basic iron and steel	Heavy structurals, transmission towers, seamless tubes, cast iron pipes, etc.
Aluminum products ex-machinery	Springs, chains, wires, etc.
Machinery except electrical	Mining, earth-moving and construction machinery, components of internal combustion engines, jute mill machinery, sugar mill machinery, tea machinery, chemical plants and other industrial machinery of several kinds
Electrical machinery	Switch gear and control gear, paper, insulated power cells
Miscellaneous manufacture	Variety of items like instruments, photographic goods, watches and clocks, etc.

Importance of Difference in Weights and Outputs in the Index of Industrial Production, China and India

For China, for the period 1949–59, alternative indexes have been computed by Liu and Yeh, Chao Kang, and R. M. Field, among others. Their indexes for 1957, with 1952 as base, are presented in table 17. While the differences in the overall indexes are not very significant, those for some of the subgroups are substantial. The index for handicrafts is an outstanding example. We cannot accept any of these indexes because of the special needs of this study. However, for the reasons given by Field,[40] I shall use his index to illustrate the importance of weights in the construction of the index of industrial production. With 1956 as base, Field's index for 1957 is 111.0 for China, and for India the index is 104.3. This difference in the rate of growth from 1956 to 1957 is due as much *to*

[40] R. M. Field, "Chinese Communist Industrial Production" (see table 17 above), pp. 279–83. In my opinion, Field's index would lead to an underestimate of the industrial rate of growth. Field, in the April-June 1970 issue (no. 42) of *China Quarterly*—after this manuscript was completed—revised his index upward. However, it is still on the low side. For a more detailed criticism, see Appendix B.

TABLE 17

THREE INDEXES OF INDUSTRIAL PRODUCTION, CHINA, 1957
(1952 = 100)

	Field (1)	Chao (2)	Liu-Yeh (3)
Total industrial production	195.1	189.9	194.2
Industry	208.8	195.9	240.2
Electric power	266.4	266.4	265.9
Coal	195.6	197.7	194.0
Petroleum	334.4	334.4	334.4
Ferrous metals	386.5	353.7	354.0
Nonferrous metals	...	370.0	...
Metal processing	241.0	...	...
Machine building	284.1	271.5	441.1
Chemical processing	312.9	314.2	277.3
Building materials	239.8	241.6	269.3
Timber	252.9	199.6	
Paper	245.6	220.1	253.9
Textiles	153.2	136.7	138.6
Food	180.2	156.2	168.7
Handicrafts	138.7	164.8	114.0

SOURCES.—Col. 1: R. M. Field, "Chinese Communist Industrial Production," in *An Economic Profile of Mainland China* (Washington, D.C.: Joint Economic Committee, U.S. Congress, 1967). Col. 2: Chao Kang, *The Rate and Pattern of Industrial Growth in Communist China* (Ann Arbor: University of Michigan Press, 1965) pp. 88, 96. Col. 3: T. C. Liu and K. C. Yeh, *The Economy of the Chinese Mainland* (Princeton, N.J.: Princeton University Press, 1965), pp. 66, 146, 573, 585. The index of total industrial production is derived from data on the value-added (in 1952 yuan) by industry and handicrafts; the value-added by industry is derived from data on factories, mining, and utilities. The indexes for electric power, coal, and petroleum are derived from the data on net value-added in ibid. (pp. 573, 585). The indexes for all other branches of industry are derived from the data on gross value-added in ibid. (p. 146). Ferrous metals is the sum of pig iron, steel, and rolled steel; building materials is the sum of cement, sheet glass, and other construction materials; textiles is the sum of cotton yarn, cotton cloth, silk piece goods, woolen textiles, grass cloth, and knitted goods; and food is the sum of sugar, milled rice, wheat flour, edible vegetable oils, and cigarettes.

differences in weight as to differences in output performance. This conclusion is supported by the following identity:

$$I^1 - I^2 = \sum w_j^2(I_j^1 - I_j^2) + \sum I_j^1(w_j^1 - w_j^2) \qquad (6)$$

where I represents the index of industrial production, w represents weight, the superscript 1 refers to China and 2 to India, and subscript j refers to commodity group.

Equation (6) suggests that the difference in the level of index of industrial production between China and India has two components: (1) the difference in output levels of various industries, weighted by Indian value-added shares; and (2) the difference between weights used in China and India, evaluated at the Chinese level of industrial production.

Nearly 48 percent of the difference between the two indices of industrial production is due to the differences in weights, and 52 percent is due to the difference in output levels (table 18). The major differences in weights arise in metal processing, building materials, timber, and textiles.

TABLE 18

INDEX OF INDUSTRIAL PRODUCTION AND ITS DISTRIBUTION BY INDUSTRIES, CHINA AND INDIA, 1957
(1956 WEIGHTS, 1956 = 100)

	Index of Industrial Production		Weights		Source of Difference in Overall Index Output		
Industry	China (1)	India (2)	China (3)	India (4)	Weight (5)	Level (6)	Total (7)
Electric power	116.6	112.8	2.6	4.0	−2.1	+0.2	−1.9
Coal	117.3	110.4	14.5	7.7	+5.4	+0.5	+5.9
Petroleum	125.4	114.3	1.1	4.1	−4.0	+0.5	−3.5
Ferrous metals	133.3	99.6	7.0	10.0	−5.3	+3.4	−1.9
Metal processing	105.5	116.4	23.5	5.0	+15.8	−0.6	+15.2
Building materials	107.3	114.6	11.6	2.7	+7.6	−0.2	+7.4
Timber	134.1	125.0	6.9	0.4	+7.2	+0.0	+7.2
Paper	125.2	109.5	1.4	1.5	−0.4	+0.2	−0.2
Textiles	94.0	99.9	24.9	45.5	−22.9	−2.7	−25.6
Food	116.2	106.4	21.1	15.2	+3.1	+1.5	+4.6
Total	111.0	104.3	100.0	100.0	+3.2	+3.5	+6.7

SOURCES.—Cols. 1 and 3: R. M. Field, "Chinese Communist Industrial Production," in *An Economic Profile of Mainland China* (Washington, D.C.: Joint Economic Committee, U.S. Congress, 1967). Cols. 2 and 4: *Statistical Abstract of the Indian Union* (New Delhi: Central Statistical Organization, 1966). Cols. 5–7: Computed by using eq. (6); the industrial distribution is of the difference between the *total* index of China and India. Thus the figures in any row show the contribution of that row to the total difference.

Except for textiles, these industries also have the lowest rupee per yuan parity ratio. The peculiarity of the Chinese price system is therefore probably accountable for the rather wide differences in weights chosen for these industries. The case of textiles is obvious.

TABLE 19

STRUCTURE OF VALUE-ADDED, CHINA AND INDIA, 1956
(CURRENT PRICES, %)

Sector	China	India
Electric power	2.18	4.01
Coal	12.26	7.72
Petroleum	0.92	4.12
Ferrous metals	5.96	10.07
Metal products	19.96	4.90
Chemical products	2.88	3.87
Building materials	9.82	2.69
Timber	5.83	0.44
Paper	1.21	1.51
Textiles	21.10	45.45
Food	17.88	15.23
Total	100.00	100.00

SOURCES.—China: R. M. Field, "Chinese Communist Industrial Production," in *an Economic Profile of Mainland China* (Washington, D.C.: Joint Economic Committee, U.S. Congress, 1967). India: *Statistical Abstract of the Indian Union* (New Delhi: Central Statistical Organization, 1967).

This problem of weights is of concern because it reflects the distortion effects of the Chinese price system. This distortion shows up not only in the index but also in the value-added shares. Table 19 shows the China and India value-added structures differ substantially. Since the production structures of Chinese and Indian economies are quite similar, the differences in the value-added structures must be due to the differences in pricing.

As already indicated, the indexes of industrial production in China and India must both be recomputed. The Chinese index used hereafter is derived from raw industrial output data. For weights, perhaps the least unacceptable procedure, given data availability uses the 1956 Indian value-added shares for both countries to ensure comparability of the two series. The Chinese value-added shares could also be used. Although the latter weights would raise the estimated rate of growth of industrial production in India, the relative performance of the two countries would not be altered. The Indian value-added weights were, however, preferred because they represent factor scarcities in the two countries less inaccurately.

For 1952–57, R. M. Field already has done considerable recomputation of the index for China, but he has used the Chinese value-added weights to compute the overall index. Since his sectoral indices are free of this drawback, I have accepted them. I then computed overall index for 1952–57 for China using Indian value-added weights of 1956.

For 1958–65 for China, the index was entirely recomputed. The outputs of representative products were converted into indices to represent sectoral indices, and combined by taking an arithmetic sum with Indian value-added weights, to derive an estimate of the overall index of industrial production. As a check on this methodology I also used it to derive an index for 1952–57. This method led to a slight overestimate of the rate of growth, since some of the products were not good "representatives." For example, chemical fertilizer had been chosen to represent the chemical industry. This representative product clearly grew at higher rates than the industry as a whole. However, since no better data on representative products were available, fertilizer was retained to represent the chemical industry. To correct the upward bias this introduces in the rate of growth, I reduced the level of the overall index. This reduction amounted to less than 1 percent in any year.[41]

For India, the scope and valuation are made complete by choosing 1956 as the base year. However, to bring the scope in line with the Chinese concept, the index of industrial production was recomputed to exclude mining and quarrying, footwear, rubber products, leather and fur

[41] This methodology is quite common in the study of Communist countries. Field has used it in his work. Earlier employers are N. Kaplan and R. H. Moorsteen, *Index of Soviet Industrial Output* (Santa Monica, Calif: RAND Corp., 1960). For further details on the industrial production statistics, see Appendix B.

products, and nonmetallic products. These sectors account for about 16 percent of industrial value-added. Other corrections were minor and were made merely to restore consistency in the production series[42] and to test its validity.

Rate of Growth of Industrial Production, 1952–70

The derivation of the index of industrial production for China for 1952–65 has already been described. Since data are available for 1966–70, I constructed the index for this period also. The computed overall and industrial indices are presented in tables 20–22. For India, as already indicated, I

TABLE 20

INDEX OF INDUSTRIAL PRODUCTION, CHINA, 1952–59
(1956 = 100; INDIA VALUE-ADDED WEIGHTS)

Sector	1952	1953	1954	1955	1956	1957	1958	1959
Electric power	43.8	55.4	66.3	73.8	100.0	116.6	165.9	250.1
Coal	60.0	62.9	75.5	88.4	100.0	117.3	179.9	234.5
Petroleum	37.5	53.5	67.8	83.1	100.0	125.4	194.7	318.1
Ferrous metals	34.5	46.2	54.9	69.1	100.0	133.3	189.4	264.1
Metal products	43.8	51.1	60.9	62.6	100.0	105.5	163.7	204.2
Chemical products	38.1	47.5	63.1	76.0	100.0	119.3	166.3	234.6
Building materials	44.8	60.6	72.0	70.4	100.0	107.3	145.5	191.9
Timber	53.0	83.3	105.9	100.1	100.0	134.1	169.0	199.6
Paper	51.0	58.6	71.1	78.8	100.0	125.2	166.9	233.1
Textiles	61.4	74.9	85.3	77.9	100.0	94.0	116.9	148.7
Food	64.5	79.0	85.6	93.2	100.0	116.2	127.3	153.0
Total	54.9	67.2	77.5	79.3	100.0	107.9	137.6	151.1

SOURCES.—The sectoral indices are from R. M. Field, "Chinese Communist Industrial Production," in *An Economic Profile of Mainland China* (Washington, D.C.: Joint Economic Committee, U.S. Congress, 1967). The total index is a weighted average with value-added shares in India, given in table 19, used as weights. For 1958 and 1959, the total index is derived by the methods described in table 22.

TABLE 21

INDEX OF INDUSTRIAL PRODUCTION, CHINA, 1960–65
(1956 = 100; BASED ON SELECTED PRODUCTION STATISTICS)

Sector	1960	1961	1962	1963	1964	1965
Electric power	287.0	165.5	142.2	155.1	181.0	201.7
Coal	326.9	192.3	153.9	192.3	160.8	176.9
Petroleum	308.2	308.2	363.0	404.1	479.5	547.9
Ferrous metals	284.5	224.3	149.5	168.2	186.9	205.6
Metal products	n.a.	n.a.	n.a.	n.a.	n.a.	n.a.
Chemical products	298.2	285.1	342.5	362.8	528.7	489.3
Building materials	196.8	87.5	87.5	102.0	116.6	131.2
Timber	139.8	121.9	103.9	100.3	121.9	114.7
Paper	200.0	216.7	225.0	233.3	241.7	250.0
Textiles	118.8	79.2	69.3	85.1	95.0	99.0
Food	104.6	93.0	104.6	110.5	131.4	158.1
Total	194.4	138.5	126.8	147.2	161.6	175.5

[42] See Subramanian Swamy, "Economic Growth and Income Distribution in a Developing Nation: The Case of India" (see n. 24 above).

TABLE 22

INDEX OF INDUSTRIAL PRODUCTION, CHINA, 1966–70
(1957 = 100; BASED ON SELECTED PRODUCTION STATISTICS)

Sector	1966	1967	1968	1969	1970
Electric power	247.3	205.2	221.0	n.a.	315.7
Coal	183.2	145.0	160.3	n.a.	194.6
Petroleum	666.7	666.7	733.3	n.a.	1333.3
Ferrous metals	222.2	185.1	222.2	n.a.	333.3
Metal products	n.a.	n.a.	n.a.	n.a.	n.a.
Chemical products	687.5	500.0	600.0	n.a.	812.5
Building materials	173.9	144.9	159.4	n.a.	195.6
Timber	135.7	121.4	128.5	n.a.	135.7
Paper	150.0	141.6	141.6	n.a.	208.3
Textiles	110.0	90.0	100.0	n.a.	170.0
Food	177.7	188.8	200.0	n.a.	188.8
Total	179.9	163.0	179.8	n.a.	240.4

SOURCE.—Table B2.

NOTES.—The indices are based on a selected sample of representative products. Crude oil represents (≡) petroleum, crude steel ≡ ferrous metals, fertilizer ≡ chemical products, cement ≡ building materials, cotton cloth ≡ textiles, sugar ≡ food. These selected commodities represent 65 percent of the commodities in table 20. Indian value-added shares for 1956 were used in deriving the total index.

adopted the scope of industrial production followed for 1956 (tables 23 and 24). However, two cautionary remarks must be made at this point. First, the period 1966–69 coincides with the Cultural Revolution in China, which by all accounts set back industrial production. Hence inclusion of this period lowers the trend growth rate of industrial production in China. Second, the crop years 1965–66 and 1966–67 in India were years of unprecedented drought, and the industrial sector suffered from a lack of agricultural raw materials and electric power. Further, because of the Indo-Pakistan War toward the end of 1965 the government of India restricted the importation of maintenance items. These two events, coupled with some bad economic policy,[43] caused a significant setback to industrial production as well as a lower rate of growth.

In view of the special situations that arose in both China and India during 1966–69, perhaps the time span for calculation of the trend growth rate to 1952–65 should be restricted. However, it can be argued that these disequilibria were a direct result of policy, and hence these years ought to be included in the analysis of industrial performance. This question has been left open here by calculating the rates of growth, including as well as excluding this period.

Before any inferences are drawn from tables 20–25, a comment is in order regarding the initial year chosen for comparison. I used 1953, whereas it is practice to use 1952 and 1948–49. The initial year was determined as the one in which the previous peak in industrial production was regained. This criterion is meaningful because both China and India were

[43] See Subramanian Swamy (*Indian Economic Planning: An Alternative Approach* [New Delhi: Vikas, 1971]) for details.

TABLE 23

INDEX OF INDUSTRIAL PRODUCTION, INDIA, 1951–65
(1956 = 100; 1956 VALUE-ADDED WEIGHTS)

Sector	1951	1952	1953	1954	1955	1956	1957	1958	1959	1960	1961	1962	1963	1964	1965
Electric power	60.9	63.7	69.0	77.4	88.1	100.0	112.8	127.4	151.4	171.0	198.8	223.4	257.9	297.2	326.5
Coal	87.0	91.9	91.0	93.6	97.0	100.0	110.4	115.1	119.3	131.3	140.1	153.8	167.2	159.9	173.6
Petroleum	6.4	6.0	6.3	16.5	77.7	100.0	114.3	122.7	132.4	147.7	156.5	169.2	196.6	217.2	231.0
Ferrous metals	83.5	85.7	81.0	95.1	96.7	100.0	99.6	106.8	138.6	183.2	181.7	225.1	259.4	260.7	271.3
Metal products	47.3	46.1	48.9	66.2	83.0	100.0	116.4	126.3	141.5	176.8	204.1	230.1	272.7	310.8	353.4
Chemical products	72.9	78.4	83.7	84.5	96.3	100.0	100.5	116.4	131.1	147.7	170.5	184.2	204.1	223.5	235.3
Building materials	64.4	69.1	70.2	80.0	87.5	100.0	114.6	128.7	146.7	168.8	181.6	221.2	205.5	217.0	233.5
Timber	55.3	62.3	70.4	82.7	87.7	100.0	110.0	105.4	137.2	147.8	150.2	169.0	200.2	202.6	237.5
Paper	66.5	69.2	72.1	81.4	95.9	100.0	109.5	127.3	145.4	173.5	182.0	191.0	226.9	237.9	255.6
Textiles	78.5	81.5	87.1	90.3	93.4	100.0	99.9	98.5	102.1	104.8	108.4	113.5	120.9	129.3	129.9
Food	79.6	84.7	82.3	81.9	93.3	100.0	106.4	107.6	109.6	117.4	129.3	127.4	122.7	135.6	144.4
Total	73.5	75.8	77.9	83.2	91.9	100.0	104.3	107.7	116.9	130.1	138.4	150.6	162.9	174.8	184.5

SOURCE: *Statistical Abstract of the Indian Union* (New Delhi: Central Statistical Organization, 1968).
NOTE.—The weights are given in table 19; the total index is a weighted average.

TABLE 24

INDEX OF INDUSTRIAL PRODUCTION, INDIA
(1956 = 100; 1956 VALUE-ADDED WEIGHTS)

Sector	1966	1967	1968	1969	1970
Electric power	355.3	394.5	455.9	514.7	584.0
Coal	177.6	180.3	190.8	199.9	188.9
Petroleum	285.0	340.9	378.8	408.5	439.9
Ferrous metals	347.3	333.0	354.8	384.2	370.8
Metal products	368.5	339.6	320.4	362.3	379.4
Chemical products	248.7	254.3	291.6	321.2	353.4
Building materials	244.2	249.3	263.8	301.0	311.9
Timber	261.3	287.4	316.1	347.7	382.5
Paper	277.6	289.9	321.0	349.6	384.5
Textiles	114.2	112.8	117.9	114.8	116.1
Food	152.1	132.0	128.2	161.9	193.2
Total	189.3	187.8	197.8	213.5	223.8

SOURCES.—*Basic Statistics relating to the Indian Economy* (New Delhi: Planning Commission, 1969); and *Economic Survey, 1970–71* (New Delhi: Ministry of Finance, 1971).

TABLE 25

INDEX OF INDUSTRIAL PRODUCTION, CHINA AND INDIA
(1956 = 100; 1956 INDIA VALUE-ADDED WEIGHTS)

Year	China	India
1951	n.a.	73.5
1952	54.9	75.8
1953	67.2	77.9
1954	77.5	83.2
1955	79.3	91.9
1956	100.0	100.0
1957	107.9	104.3
1958	137.6	107.7
1959	191.1	116.9
1960	194.4	130.1
1961	138.5	138.4
1962	126.8	150.6
1963	147.2	162.9
1964	161.6	174.8
1965	175.5	184.5
1966	194.1	189.3
1967	175.8	187.8
1968	194.0	197.8
1969	n.a.	213.5
1970	259.3	223.8
Average:		
1953–57	86.4	91.5
1958–60	174.4	118.2
1962–66	161.0	172.4
1966–70	205.8	202.4

SOURCES.—Tables 20–24.

involved in World War II and subject to serious internal disruption thereafter.[44] Hence we must distinguish between *growth* and *recovery*. Evidence suggests that the 1943 peak in India was regained in 1952–53, and the 1937 peak in China was regained in 1953.

On the basis of the evidence in table 26, the following observations are tenable. First, the overall rate of growth during 1953–66 of industrial

TABLE 26

RATE OF GROWTH OF INDUSTRIAL PRODUCTION, CHINA AND INDIA (% PER YEAR)

Period	China	India
1953–57 to 1958–60	17.6	6.6
1958–60 to 1962–66	−1.6	7.4
1962–66 to 1966–70	6.1	4.0
1953–57 to 1962–66	6.9	7.1
1953–57 to 1966–70	6.7	6.1

production is about 7.0 percent per year, roughly the same in both countries. This rate is not impressive, since several developing nations have experienced much higher rates of growth during the same period. If the terminal year is shifted to 1970, the Chinese growth rate is slightly higher than the Indian. The drought and the Indo-Pakistan War caused the Indian growth rate to drop to 4.0 percent during 1966–70. Since "high" estimates have been used for China, the two rates of growth are probably quite similar. If the estimates of Perkins, Liu, and Cheng had been used, the estimated Chinese industrial growth would have been even smaller.[45]

The second observation is that from 1953 to 1966 the rate of industrial progress in China retarded significantly: from 17.6 percent to −1.6 percent. In India, on the other hand, the rate of growth accelerated markedly: from 6.6 percent to 7.4 percent. Thus, while the overall 1953–66 rates of growth of industrial production are not very different, the component trends are, in fact, diametrically different.

There are, of course, good reasons for these trends. Until 1965 India was making a systematic though undramatic effort to plan her industrialization. While many serious errors of judgment and understanding were made, the basic fiber of the Indian system was sound, permitting steady growth and acceleration. In China, the situation was entirely different. The supremacy of politics over economics caused several major dislocations. The Big Leap Forward, rapid commune formation, severe drought,

[44] Because of Three-Anti and Five-Anti movements in 1951–52, the industrial production levels in 1952 were considerably depressed in China.

[45] My estimates are supported by the data given by Chou En-lai to Edgar Snow in 1971. According to Premier Chou, the industrial production value in 1970 was approximately 211 billion yuan. Comparing this with the official figures for 1957, the compound rate of industrial production value is 7.6 percent per year. Compared with 1958, the annual compound rate of growth is 7.0 percent, quite close to the 6.7 percent per year estimated here. Also, the officially estimated rate of growth (*Ten Great Years* [Wei Dah de Shyr Nian] [Peking: Statistical Publishing House, 1959]) for the 1950s is 18.0 percent, again close to my estimate of 17.6 percent.

and the sudden cutoff of USSR assistance combined to make 1959–62 crisis years, necessitating the abandonment of two successive 5-year plans.

The sectoral structure of industrial growth is shown in table 27. Although adequate data for China are available only for 1957–65, information for other years on representative products confirms the findings in the table.

TABLE 27

SECTORAL CONTRIBUTION TO INDUSTRIAL GROWTH, CHINA AND INDIA

(%)

Sector	China (1953–57)	India (1951–65)
Electric power	5.29	7.75
Coal	9.80	3.11
Petroleum	6.16	15.54
Ferrous metals	15.79	13.28
Metal products	6.37	12.10
Chemical products	5.62	4.52
Building materials	3.24	3.78
Timber	0.61	0.82
Paper	2.13	2.22
Textiles	29.75	23.31
Food	15.22	13.57
Total	100.00	100.00

SOURCES.—Tables 20 and 23.

NOTE.—The methodology used is embodied in the following equation:

$$I = \sum_{i=1}^{11} w_i I_i \cdot (\Delta I_j / I_i)$$

About 57 percent of the total industrial growth in both China and India was due to two modern sectors (electric power and metal products) and two traditional ones (namely, textiles and food). If petroleum and ferrous metals are included, almost 80 percent of the industrial growth in China and over 85 percent in India was accounted for by these six sectors. The growth of textiles and food industries reflects the growing urbanization and marketization in both countries. Since electric power and metal products are key sectors of industrial growth, they have received much attention in the economic planning of China and India. Petroleum and ferrous metals are important input supplying industries, and without their expansion rapid growth in other sectors is impossible.

Net Value-added in Industry, China, 1952–70

The "industry" sector includes three types of production units: (1) factory establishments; (2) handicraft production units; and (3) construction, mining, and utilities. To estimate the value-added in industry, these three types are treated separately, adjusting gross value of output for input costs and depreciation.

Chinese official publications do not indicate the number of trial commodities included in their estimate of gross value of output of factory establishments. It is known that the official industrial classification recognizes twenty-one major industrial sectors and 250 subsectors, but this knowledge obviously is inadequate. Hence, I had to construct my own estimate of net value-added for factory establishments; and I followed the method of Liu and Yeh but used some significant differences in scope and netness.

Net Value-added, 1952–57

The index of industrial production was based on the output of thirty-one commodities for which official data are available.[46] These data were cross-checked with other sources, official and nonofficial.[47] Gross value of output for these thirty-one commodities were then estimated by means of the price data of Liu and Yeh and of others. By subtracting this figure from the officially published figures[48] for presumably more than thirty-one commodities, we obtained the gross value of output for the residual unidentified commodities. This residual category accounted for about 22 percent of total gross value. It is here that the basic differences with Liu and Yeh arise. They feel that the rate of growth of the "unidentified" consumer goods is too high to be realistic; and they replace this unidentified series by one with the same rate of growth as that for the identified series. They give no specific reason for the change, except to say that the share of the gross value of unidentified consumer goods in the total gross value rises sharply from 26 percent in 1952 to 42 percent in 1957. In my view, there are no substantive reasons for the change. If the official estimates for the identified set (31 here, 26 in Liu-Yeh) are accepted as correct, the official figures for the unidentified should also be as correct.

From the gross value of output published officially, but adjusted for scope, the gross value-added of factory establishments is estimated by a simple procedure: the 1933 ratio of gross value-added to gross value of output is applied to the 1952–57 figures. From gross value-added deduct 13 percent, net value-added. The estimates thus obtained are very close to Liu and Yeh's calculation of "adjusted" official Chinese (which is simply the official figures adjusted for the scope biases enumerated earlier), and not surprisingly since my basic disagreement with Liu and Yeh is over the items of data bias. Therefore, instead of adding another marginally different estimate, I have used the "adjusted" (not Liu-Yeh's) estimates. The summary calculation of the net value-added for factory establishments is given in table 28.

Net value-added of the industrial sector is shown in table 29. For the handicraft component of industrial production, the "adjusted" estimate

[46] Chen Nai-ruenn (see n. 34 above), pp. 186–88.

[47] Though our index for 1952–57 used Field's data, differences in output were present. For coal and chemical fertilizer, e.g., we did not accept Field's figures.

[48] From Chen Nai-ruenn (see n. 34 above), p. 207, adjusted for scope difference.

TABLE 28

Calculation of Net Value-added by Factory Establishments, 1952–57 (1952 Prices; Billion Yuan)

Item	1952	1953	1954	1955	1956	1957
1. Gross value of industrial production.........	27.01	35.58	41.52	44.75	58.67	65.02
2. Scope misclassification.	6.74	8.62	9.84	10.93	11.41	13.64
3. Adjusted gross value	20.27	26.96	31.68	33.82	47.26	51.38
4. Gross value-added	7.46	9.99	11.73	12.62	18.05	19.83
5. Depreciation	1.01	1.35	1.58	1.69	2.36	2.57
6. Net value-added....	6.45	8.64	10.15	10.93	15.69	17.26

Source.—Line 1: Official Chinese sources contained in Chen Nai-ruenn, *Chinese Economic Statistics* (Chicago: Aldine Publishing Co., 1966), pp. 208–11, esp. table 4.39. Line 2: Correction for concept of *gong chaang faa*; exclusion of modern mining, electric power, timber, handicraft, water supply and gas, and fishery products; and inclusion of pig iron and cotton yarn. For a full description, see T. C. Liu and K. C. Yeh, *The Economy of the Chinese Mainland* (Princeton, N.J.: Princeton University Press, 1965), pp. 452 et seq. Line 3: Deflated by the ratio of gross value-added to gross value in 1933. In deflation, a distinction is made between producer and consumer goods. Line 4: See text. Line 5: 5 percent of line 3.

has also been accepted.[49] Data on handicrafts in all countries are quite poor, but in China these pose a special problem because Chinese statisticians seem to have been of two minds about the appropriate classification of handicrafts. Hence I made no detailed calculations and, in fact, accepted the "adjusted" estimates. I did, however, increase the 1952–55 figures by 3.06 billion yuan annually to correct for underreporting before socialization in 1956.

TABLE 29

Net Value-added in Industrial Sector, China, 1952–57 (Constant 1952 Prices; Billion Yuan)

Item	1952	1953	1954	1955	1956	1957
Net value-added, factory	6.45	8.64	10.15	10.93	15.69	17.26
Net value-added, handicraft	4.41	4.45	4.59	4.94	5.20	5.73
Net value-added, mining, construction, and utilities	3.61	4.11	4.93	5.73	7.94	8.40
Net value-added, industry	14.47	17.20	19.67	21.60	28.83	31.39
Net value-added, industry, corrected	17.53	20.06	22.63	24.66	28.83	31.39

Sources.—See table 28, and text. The correction carried out in line 5, for 1952–55, is for underestimation. Industrial output of roughly 3.06 billion yuan, which was outside the Chinese statistical system before, was included in 1956 after socialization.

[49] The term "adjusted" is taken throughout this study to mean official Chinese figures adjusted for scope biases.

TABLE 30

NET VALUE-ADDED IN INDUSTRIAL SECTOR, CHINA
(1952 PRICES; BILLION YUAN)

Item	1958	1959	1960	1961	1962	1963	1964	1965	1970
1. Adjusted gross value factory	68.80	92.68	94.28	67.17	61.50	71.39	78.38	85.12	125.76
2. Gross value-added, factory	26.56	35.77	36.39	25.93	23.74	27.56	30.25	32.86	48.54
3. Depreciation (13% line 2)	3.44	4.63	4.71	3.36	3.08	3.56	3.92	4.26	6.29
4. Net value-added, factory (lines 2–3)	23.12	31.14	31.68	22.57	20.66	24.00	26.33	28.60	42.35
5. Gross value, handicrafts	13.48	16.31	16.59	10.48	8.36	9.00	8.70	9.45	12.58
6. Gross value-added, handicrafts	7.48	8.73	8.88	6.16	5.43	5.29	5.11	5.56	6.98
7. Depreciation (8% line 6)	0.60	0.70	0.71	0.49	0.43	0.42	0.41	0.45	0.56
8. Net value-added, industries (lines 4 + 9)	30.00	39.17	39.85	28.24	27.66	28.87	31.03	33.71	48.77
9. Net value-added, handicrafts (lines 6-7)	6.88	8.03	8.17	5.67	5.00	4.87	4.70	5.11	6.42
10. Net value-added, construction, utilities, and mining	11.01	15.29	15.56	10.75	9.84	11.42	12.54	13.19	19.49
11. Net value-added, industrial sector (lines 8 + 10)	41.01	54.46	55.41	38.99	37.50	40.29	43.57	46.90	68.26

SOURCES.—Line 1: Approximately 0.485 × index of industrial production in table 25. Line 2: Approximately 0.386 × line 1. Line 5: k_t × line 1, where k_t for 1958–62 is obtained from Yuan Tay-shu, "The Handicraft Industry and Its Economic Form," *Jing Jih Yan Jiou* (Peking), no. 7 (1962), p. 5. The k-value for 1963–64 is obtained from T'ien P'ing, "Great Strides in Handicraft Production" (source given in R. M. Field, "Industrial Production in Communist China," in *An Economic Profile of Mainland China* [Washington, D.C.: Joint Economic Committee, U.S. Congress, 1967]). The 1965–70 values for k are extrapolated. Line 6: obtained by applying the 1952–57 ratio of gross value to gross value-added figures. Line 10: Same method as described for line 5.

Net Value-added, 1958–70

Acceptable estimates of Chinese industrial output in 1958–70 are even more difficult to derive. However, I made a tentative estimate of value-added for the industrial sector by correlating the components of value-added with the available indexes of industrial production. While this estimate of value-added is probably less reliable than the estimate of value-added in agriculture, it does reflect reasonably well the trend of industrial production. My projected estimate for 1970, of net value-added in industry, is 68.26 billion yuan, or about one-third of gross value of industrial production (see table 30). Premier Chou En-lai told Edgar Snow in February 1971 that the 1970 *gross* value of industrial production was 211.0 billion yuan. About one-third of this, 70 billion yuan, represents the *net* value-added in industry. Since the official estimate of 70 billion yuan is close to my estimate of 68.26 billion yuan, it imparts some validity to the estimation procedure employed. Furthermore, according to my method, the ratio of gross value-added to gross value of industrial production is around 35 percent, and it also agrees with the official figure.[50]

Output figures for factories are available for only ten commodities and were obtained by scholars only after painstaking research. Output of these ten commodities is hardly an adequate basis for reliable estimates of value-added in industry. Therefore, we estimated factory establishment gross value of industrial production by regressing[51] gross value against the index of industrial production given in table 25. Gross value-added of factory establishments was derived by deflating gross value by the ratio for 1952–57 of gross value-added to gross value of output for factory establishments. Depreciation was then estimated, as for 1952–57, at roughly 13 percent of gross value-added.

To estimate the handicrafts output, a time series of the ratio of handicrafts to total industrial production was obtained from official Chinese sources. We applied ratio to the gross value of handicrafts production.[52] Then, by means of the ratio of gross value to gross value-added in handicrafts during 1952–57, the gross value-added was estimated. Taking a depreciation of 8 percent of gross value-added, the net value-added of handicrafts was obtained.

The estimate of net value-added of utilities, construction, and mining was also derived by postulating a time-variant relationship between their gross value and the gross value of industrial production. Since these sectors are essentially ancillaries to factory establishment, this assumption cannot be intolerably off the mark.

[50] "Several Problems of Computing the Gross Value of Industrial Output" (see n. 35 above).

[51] The 1970 figure is not estimated by this technique but is the figure that Chou En-lai gave Edgar Snow in early 1971.

[52] Since value of factory and handicrafts added to total value of industrial production, the appropriate ratio to be applied is easily derivable from the ratio described in the text.

Net Value-added in Industry, India, 1952–70

The calculation of the net value-added aggregates for India is similar to that for China. The supply of data is much greater for India, since there are not only a periodic Census of Manufacturers and Annual Surveys of Industries but also by-product government statistics. Moreover, since the Central Statistical Organization attempts to adhere to norms set by the United Nations, an acceptable estimate of net value-added is more easily calculated.

The problems of scope, valuation, and comparability that do exist have been examined in some detail elsewhere.[53] Therefore the corrected value-added shares are presented without further discussion.

For presentation in table 31, net value-added for the industrial sector *as a whole* has been multiplied by the parity rate (0.98 yuan = 1 rupee; see table 32).

TABLE 31

NET VALUE-ADDED IN INDUSTRIAL SECTOR, CHINA AND INDIA (CONSTANT PRICES; BILLION PARITY RUPEES)

	China		India	
Year	Net Value 1952 Prices	Annual Growth (%)	Net Value 1948–49 Prices	Annual Growth (%)
1952	17.2	...	15.2	...
1953	19.5	13.4	15.8	4.0
1954	21.7	11.3	16.5	4.4
1955	23.3	7.4	17.0	3.0
1956	29.6	27.0	17.6	3.5
1957	31.5	6.4	18.4	4.5
1958	40.2	27.6	18.6	1.1
1959	53.4	32.8	18.8	1.1
1960	54.3	1.7	19.7	4.8
1961	38.2	−29.7	21.1	7.1
1962	36.8	−3.7	22.1	4.7
1963	39.5	7.3	23.0	4.1
1964	42.7	8.1	24.4	6.1
1965	46.0	7.7	25.3	3.7
1970	66.9	...	30.2	...

SOURCES.—China: 1952–57—Table 29. 1958–70—Table 30. The yuan figures are converted to parity rupees at the rates given below. India: 1952–58—*Estimates of National Income and Product*, Conventional Series (New Delhi: Central Statistical Organization, 1971); 1959–70 are from *Economic Survey, 1970–71* (New Delhi: Ministry of Finance, 1971).

According to table 32, the rate of growth of net value-added in industry is significantly larger in China than in India. Although the rate of growth of factory output is about the same in both countries, about 7.0 percent per year from 1952 to 1965 (see table 26), the rate of growth of net value-added in industry is markedly different. The main reason for this finding is the relatively poor performance in India of the nonfactory industrial sector. This can be easily illustrated. The production of factory

[53] Subramanian Swamy, "Economic Growth and Income Distribution in a Developing Nation: The Case of India" (see n. 24 above).

TABLE 32

RATE OF GROWTH OF NET VALUE-ADDED IN INDUSTRY, CHINA AND INDIA (% PER YEAR)

Period	China	India
1952–56 to 1957–59..............	15.4	3.1
1957–59 to 1961–65..............	−0.3	4.4
1961–65 to 1970.................	7.1	3.8
1952–56 to 1961–65..............	6.6	3.8
1952–56 to 1970.................	6.8	3.8

establishment net output to net output industry is 53 percent in China and 22 percent in India. Small industries and handicrafts constitute 12 percent of industry in China and 28 percent in India. The remainder, largely mining, construction, trade, and transport, constitutes 35 percent in China and 50 percent in India. The rates of growth for 1952–65 of these subsectors are: factory establishments—6.9 percent in China, 7.1 percent in India; small industries and handicraft—6.9 percent in China, 1.3 percent in India; and other industries—6.4 percent in China, 4.0 percent in India. In other words, the rate of growth of net value-added in industry in China is $(0.069 \times 0.53) + (0.069 \times 0.12) + (0.064 \times 0.34)$, or $6.9 \times 0.53 + 6.9 \times 0.12 = 6.7$ percent. In India, the rate of growth equals $(0.07 \times 0.22) + (0.013 \times 0.28) + (0.040 \times 0.050)$, or 3.9 percent per year.

Because of the differences in weights of the subsectors and the differential rates of growth of these subsectors, the growth rate of net value-added in industry differs markedly between China and India. Because of the lower weight of factory output in India's net industrial value-added and despite the similar factory output growth rates in China and India, the net value-added in industry has grown at a relatively faster rate in China. If we recalculate the growth rate in India using Chinese proportions, the Indian growth rate of net value-added in industry rises from 3.8 percent to 5.3 percent, much closer to the growth in China of about 6.6 percent per year. Why, then, is the weight of factory output so much lower in India than in China? Even in 1952 India was producing only half the factory output of China. In 1947, when India became free, it was not even producing domestically such rudimentary items as pencils. True, India had a steel mill which produced 100,000 tons of steel, and it had several textile mills, but the growth of these two industries has a historical specificity. Otherwise there was little else. On the other hand, China had and has relatively poor trade and transport sectors. By virtue of the small size of these sectors, factory output is proportionately larger.

Another reason for the lower net value-added growth rates in India is the poor performance of small industries and handicrafts. This is not surprising, since total public investment in these sectors has been declining, and licensing and controls discriminate against them. If the small industries sector had grown at rates comparable with those of the factory output (as they did in China), other things remaining the same, the growth rate in India would have been 5.6 percent per year instead of 3.8 percent. If both the sectoral weights and the growth rate of small industries are changed, the growth rate of net industrial value-added in India would be 6.1 percent per year, not very different from the Chinese rate of 6.6 percent per year.

In other words, the difference in net value-added growth rates (6.6 percent in China and 3.8 percent in India) is due partly to the difference in the weight of the factory establishments of industrial output and partly to the growth rate of small industries and handicrafts.[54]

Table 32 also shows that the Chinese industrial rate of growth has declined sharply. It dropped from 15.4 percent to −0.3 percent mainly because of the failure of the Great Leap, the Drought, and *sudden* termination of USSR technical aid, although in the late 1960s there was some recovery. In India, on the other hand, accelerations and decelerations are not striking: the rate accelerates in the earlier period from 3.1 percent to 4.4 percent and decelerates in the later period from 4.4 percent to 3.8 percent (mainly due to the Drought of 1966/67 and some bad economic policy initiated in 1966).[55] In fact, over the entire period from 1953 to 1970 industrial output *never declined* (see table 31).

These comparative results are based upon the most favorable estimates for China. In fact, our rates of growth are close to the estimates provided by official sources. Several students of China believe that the official figures are overestimates. Acceptance of their opinion would not materially alter the conclusions of this study; it would, in fact, strengthen them.

Appendix B
A Note on R. M. Field's Index of Industrial Production in China, 1952–68

R. M. Field has done considerable work on the index of industrial production. However, I feel that some of his estimates of industrial output are too low. I support his methodology in the construction of the overall index but not his value-added shares.

To judge the validity of his output estimates, several cross-checks were performed.[56] Some of his output figures are not consistent with other acceptable figures. First, it has been found, on the basis of the 1952–57 official figures, that the cotton output and cotton cloth production statistics are internally

[54] I may have overstated the weight of factory output in China since *I have not* calculated total industrial output in parity rupees by aggregating the subsectoral outputs valued in parity rupees. Since factory output is likely to be capital goods mainly and small industries and handicrafts mainly consumer goods, Chinese prices would produce too large a weight for factory output, which cannot be corrected for at aggregate levels.

[55] Subramanian Swamy, *Indian Economic Planning: An Alternative Approach* (see n. 43 above), esp. chap. 4.

[56] See U.S., Congress, House, Joint Economic Committee, *Mainland China in the World Economy*, 90th Cong., 1st sess., April 5–12, 1967. However, after this manuscript was completed, Field's upward revised figures confirming my criticisms of his earlier estimate were published (see R. M. Field, "Industrial Production in Communist China: 1958–65," *China Quarterly*, no. 42 [April-June 1970]).

TABLE B1

OUTPUT OF SELECTED INDUSTRIAL COMMODITIES, CHINA, 1960–65

Commodity	Unit	1960	1961	1962	1963	1964	1965
Electric power	Billion kilowatt hours	55.50	32.00	27.50	30.00	35.00	39.00
Coal	MMT	425.00	250.00	200.00	250.00	209.00	230.00
Crude oil	MMT	4.50	4.50	5.30	5.90	7.00	8.00
Crude steel	MMT	15.22	12.00	8.00	9.00	10.00	11.00
Chemical fertilizer	MMT	2.81	2.68	3.22	3.41	4.97	4.60
Cement	MMT	13.50	6.00	6.00	7.00	8.00	9.00
Timber	Million cubic meters	39.00	34.00	29.00	28.00	34.00	32.00
Paper	MMT	2.40	2.60	2.70	2.80	2.90	3.00
Cotton cloth	Billion linear meters	6.00	4.00	3.50	4.30	4.80	5.00
Sugar	MMT	0.90	0.80	0.90	0.95	1.13	1.36

SOURCES.—Crude oil, crude steel, and cement: R. M. Field, "Chinese Communist Industrial Production," in *An Economic Profile of Mainland China* (Washington, D.C.: Joint Economic Committee, U.S. Congress, 1967). Cotton cloth, sugar, and electric power: *Feei Jing Yan Jiou*, nos. 4, 6, 9 (1967). Coal, paper, and timber: *Chinese Communist Affairs*, no. 4 (1967). Chemical fertilizer: Shahid J. Burki, *A Study of Communes*, East Asia Monographs (Cambridge, Mass.: Harvard University Press, 1969), p. 6. These sources have been cross-checked with others providing isolated estimates, such as S. D. Richardson, *Forestry in Communist China* (Baltimore: Johns Hopkins, 1966); *Current Scene* (various issues); and Kao Kuang-chien, "Big Strides in China's Chemical Fertilizer Industry," *Jing Jih Daw Baw*, March 15, 1965, p. 15.

consistent with each other and with the statistics of acreage, labor force, and spindleage.[57] We may, therefore, accept the Chinese official claims of cotton production. Implicit in these production figures are the output statistics of cotton cloth in linear meters, which are substantially larger than Field's estimates. Since the quoted source in table 22 provides estimates that are close to the *implicit* official figures, those estimates have been used in this study. Second, I believe that Field's estimates of chemical fertilizer output are too low, since, given our foodgrain output figures, they imply a very high marginal product of fertilizer. The estimates I used for 1960–64 are official Chinese, obtained from the source given in table 22. Third, Field's estimate for electric power is not consistent with the output of coal and other related statistics. A consistent series is available,[58] and I used it. Tables B1 and B2 summarize the estimates used.[59]

TABLE B2

OUTPUT OF SELECTED INDUSTRIAL COMMODITIES, CHINA, 1966–70

Commodity	Unit	1966	1967	1968	1969	1970
Electric power	Billion kilowatt hours	47	39	42	62	60
Coal	MMT	240	190	210	220	255
Crude oil	MMT	10	10	11	13	20
Crude steel	MMT	12	10	12	13	18
Chemical fertilizer	MMT	5.5	4.0	4.8	n.a.	6.5
Cement	MMT	12	10	11	n.a.	13.5
Timber	Million cubic meters	38	34	36	n.a.	38
Paper	MMT	1.8	1.7	1.7	n.a.	2.5
Cotton cloth	Billion linear meters	5.5	4.5	5.0	n.a.	8.5
Sugar	MMT	1.6	1.7	1.8	n.a.	1.7

SOURCES.—1966–68: R. M. Field, "Industrial Production in Communist China: 1958–65," *China Quarterly*, no. 42 (April-June 1970). 1969: *Pravda*, May 18, 1970. 1970: Crude oil and cotton cloth—Chou En-lai as quoted by Edgar Snow, *Epoca*, February 28, 1971. Electric power, coal, fertilizer, cement, paper, and sugar—Werner Klatt, "A Review of China's Economy in 1970," *China Quarterly*, no. 42 (July-September 1970). Steel: *Mainichi*, June 24, 1971.

Appendix C
Comparison of Various Estimates of the Index of Industrial Production in China, 1952–68

Liu and Yeh, Chao, and Field, among others, have estimated the index of industrial production. We present their estimates in tables C1 and C2 and compare them with ours.

[57] R. Q. P. Chin, "The Validity of Mainland China's Cotton Textile Statistics," *Southern Economic Journal*, vol. 3 (1968).

[58] "Communist China's Electric Power Industry," *Feei Jing Yan Jiou*, vol. 4 (1967).

[59] In these tables, we show no estimate of metal products since it is difficult to select a representative product. However, an index of machinery output is available which could have been used in the derivation of the index of industrial production. It was not used because we wanted to retain Field's methodology. If the machinery output index had been incorporated, the growth rate of total industrial production would have been lowered. For the machinery index, see Cheng Chu-yuan, "Growth and Structural Change in Chinese Machine Building Industry, 1952–66," *China Quarterly*, no. 41 (January-March 1970).

My index of the physical output of industrial production shows a lower rate of growth than Field's but about the same rate as Kang Chao's index. My index for 1952–57, however, is based on the same data as Field's. The differences between the two for 1952–57 are primarily due to the weights used.

For the years 1958–65, the only other estimate is Field's (table C2). In this period, unlike 1952–57, my index shows a much higher rate of growth than Field's original estimate.

TABLE C1

VARIOUS INDICES OF INDUSTRIAL PRODUCTION EXCLUDING HANDICRAFTS, CHINA (1952 = 100)

YEAR	PHYSICAL OUTPUT INDEX			VALUE-ADDED INDEX	
	Swamy (1)	Chao (2)	Field (3)	Swamy (4)	Liu-Yeh (5)
1952..........	100	100	100	100	100
1953..........	122.4	124.7	122.7	133.0	122.9
1954..........	141.1	141.6	143.0	157.3	142.2
1955..........	144.4	146.9	148.3	169.4	159.0
1956..........	182.1	182.2	188.2	243.1	210.8
1957..........	196.5	195.9	208.8	267.5	238.6

SOURCES.—Col. 1: Table 25. Col. 2: Chao Kang, *The Rate and Pattern of Industrial Growth in Communist China* (Ann Arbor: University of Michigan Press, 1965). Col. 3: R. M. Field, "Chinese Communist Industrial Production," in *An Economic Profile of Mainland China* (Washington, D.C.: Joint Economic Committee, U.S. Congress, 1967). Col. 4: Table 29. Col. 5: T. C. Liu and K. C. Yeh, *The Economy of the Chinese Mainland* (Princeton, N.J.: Princeton University Press, 1965).

TABLE C2

TWO INDICES OF INDUSTRIAL PRODUCTION, CHINA

Year	Swamy (1)	Field (2)	Field Revised (3)
1958......................	128	131	131
1959......................	177	166	166
1960......................	180	172	162–164
1961......................	128	114	104–106
1962......................	118	100	104–106
1963......................	136	110	115–121
1964......................	150	123	130–138
1965......................	163	135	147–159
1966......................	180	n.a.	160–175
1967......................	163	n.a.	135–150
1968......................	180	n.a.	148–167

SOURCES.—Col. 1: Table 25. Col. 2: R. M. Field: "Chinese Communist Industrial Production," in *An Economic Profile of Mainland China* (Washington, D.C.: Joint Economic Committee, U.S. Congress, 1967). Col. 3: R. M. Field, "Industrial Production in Communist China: 1958–65," *China Quarterly*, no. 43 (July-September 1970).

IV. National Product and the Rate of Growth

Introduction

On the basis of the figures for net value-added for agriculture and industry, we can now estimate total product. However, before this is done, two problems must be resolved: (1) acceptable estimates of "trade" and "services" product are needed for the estimate of the product of the "residual" sector, and (2) suitable weights must be established for the combination of the sectoral estimates.

Estimates of Net Value-added in the Residual Sector, 1952–70

Needless to say, the derivation of the residual product, the net value-added in the "trade (including banking)" and "services" sector, is a difficult task, and in fact the estimates are more tenuous than those for agriculture and industry, since the statistics on trade and services have a shorter history of collection and collation in both countries.

For 1952–57 for China, the Liu-Yeh "adjusted," that is, official figures adjusted for scope biases, have been accepted. For 1958–65, the product of this sector has been estimated as a residual, that is, the net domestic product is first estimated from a linear-predictor relation of current net value-added in agriculture and a proxy variable for industry (which is lagged net value-added in agriculture) to net domestic product. All the values are in constant-parity rupees. From the estimated net domestic product, we subtracted the net value-added in agriculture and industry to obtain the residual net value-added of the trade and services sector. This estimate probably has greater validity than one based on currently available data for the residual sector, since the latter are, at present, partial and to some extent misleading. As a test of the procedure, we followed it for India, and the results provided a good fit to independently estimated (by the CSO) net domestic product and residual product. This is not surprising, since agriculture's share in total product predominates and the industrial sector has grown.[60] Another check of the estima-

[60] Su Hsinq has shown the quantitative importance of the agricultural sector in the industrial growth rate in China (see Su Hsinq, "The Two-Way Struggle between Socialism and Capitalism in China's Rural Areas after Land Reform: I, II, III," *Chinese Economic Studies* [trans.], vol. 1, no. 4 [1968]; and vol. 2, nos. 1 and 2 [1968–69]).

ted residual product is the statement made by Premier Chou En-lai.[61] According to Chou, the number of officials in the Chinese government dropped from 60,000 to 10,000 as a result of the Cultural Revolution. Other official Chinese publications indicate that the Cultural Revolution had a similar impact on other services, such as those of teachers, shop assistants, barbers, etc. It is reasonable to conclude that the total effect of the Cultural Revolution was a sharp decline in the net value-added of the trade and services sector. Since the combined services sector is likely to have an intersectoral impact on agriculture, it should affect the predictor equation and consequently show up in the estimate of residual product.

The output of the residual sector also probably declined during the drought of 1960–61. If my methodology has any validity, it should reflect these changes in trend.

Table 33 gives the net value-added estimates of the residual sector for China and India. The figures for India are from official national accounts tables. The estimated residual product series does reflect the expected

TABLE 33

NET VALUE-ADDED IN RESIDUAL SECTOR, CHINA AND INDIA (CONSTANT PRICES; BILLION PARITY RUPEES)

	China		India	
Year	Net Value-added (1952 Prices) (1)	Annual Change (%) (2)	Net Value-added (1948–49 Prices) (3)	Annual Change (%) (4)
1952	50.34	...	31.6	...
1953	52.00	3.3	32.9	4.1
1954	54.14	4.1	34.0	3.3
1955	56.11	3.6	35.5	4.4
1956	58.05	3.5	37.0	4.2
1957	59.92	3.2	39.0	5.4
1958	58.40	−2.5	40.3	3.3
1959	46.86	−19.8	42.3	5.0
1960	32.02	−31.7	44.1	4.3
1961	49.15	53.5	47.8	8.4
1962	55.71	13.3	50.1	4.8
1963	61.43	10.3	53.0	5.8
1964	66.01	7.5	56.5	6.6
1965	65.39	−0.1	60.7	7.4
1970	45.91	...	72.5	...
Averages:				
1952–56	54.13	...	34.6	...
1957–59	55.06	...	36.2	...
1961–65	59.54	...	39.1	...
1970	45.91	...	40.6	...

SOURCES.—Col. 1: 1952–57—T. C. Liu and K. C. Yeh, *The Economy of the Chinese Mainland*, (Princeton, N.J.: Princeton University Press, 1965). The "adjusted" estimates are converted to parity rupees by multiplying by 2.20 (official rate is 1 yuan = 2.00 rupees). 1958–70—See text. Col. 3: *Estimates of National Income and Product*, Conventional Series (New Delhi: Central Statistical Organization, 1971); and *Economic Survey, 1970–71* (New Delhi: Ministry of Finance, 1971).

[61] Interview with Edgar Snow, *Epoca*, February 28, 1971.

trends in China for 1960–61 and 1965–70. The table also shows that net value-added of the combined services (trade and services) is larger in China than in India, for all years except 1970.

However, although the residual sector is larger in China than India, its rate of growth is much higher in India (see table 34). The growth rate

TABLE 34

RATE OF GROWTH OF NET VALUE-ADDED IN RESIDUAL SECTOR, CHINA AND INDIA

Period	China	India
1952–56 to 1957–59	0.4	4.3
1957–59 to 1961–65	1.6	5.6
1961–65 to 1970	−3.7	4.3
1952–57 to 1961–65	1.1	5.0
1952–57 to 1970	−1.0	4.7

SOURCE.—Table 33.

in the 1950s is ten times larger in India than in China. Although the Chinese rate quadruples in the early 1950s, the Indian rate is still 3½ times the Chinese rate during that period.

The growth rate of the net value-added in this sector is much higher than the growth rate of net domestic product in India (5.0 percent vs. 3.6 percent in 1952–65) and much lower than the growth rate in China (1.1 percent). In fact, in India the residual sector's growth rate is also higher than the growth rates of the agricultural and industrial sectors. In China, on the other hand, the residual sector's growth rate is lower than those of net domestic product, net value-added in agriculture, and net value-added in industry. Why this should be so is not clear. It may just be a reflection of a growing bureaucracy in India and of the bureaucratic purges in China.

The Problem of Valuation

The second problem—that is, the choice of weights by which to combine agriculture and nonagricultural value-added to obtain national income—is the well-known valuation problem. It has concerned economists, especially those engaged in comparative work, for several years.[62] In this connection, two basic questions have to be examined before any valid comparison between China and India can be made. The first is the problem of conversion of yuans into rupees, or vice versa. The foreign exchange rate deals primarily with goods that enter international trade and is unacceptable for three reasons. First, these are two large countries with very small foreign trade proportions. Second, the official Chinese foreign exchange rate is not even remotely an equilibrium rate but has been arbitrarily pegged, and no doubt the Indian rate is also pegged. Third,

[62] Abram Bergson, *Soviet National Income since 1928* (Cambridge, Mass.: Harvard University Press, 1961), chap. 4.

China's domestic price structure does not reflect the domestic factor scarcities and marginal utilities. These prices therefore do not reflect society's weights but are primarily instruments for collecting revenue.[63]

An eminent student of China, Shigeru Ishikawa, notes: "On the basis of these points, it may be observed that prices in China are not meaningful, and hence the national income or the national total increment of *use-value* measured by such prices is not effective either in indicating a true picture of its internal structure or in making intertemporal or international comparisons, although the degree of bias involved in measurement seems not as much as in the case of the Soviet Union."[64] The Indian price structure also does not reflect the Pareto-optimal conditions, but since it is based on market determined prices it is most likely to reflect factor scarcities and marginal utilities in an approximate way.

The second major problem is the choice of a base year for the constant-price estimates. At present, 1948–49 is used for India, and Chinese figures are always given in constant 1952 prices. I have adopted these base years.

One possible solution to the first problem is to calculate the parity rates between China and India based on wholesale prices, retail prices, and foreign trade prices. Although the price data are scarce, some material is available. Table 35 summarizes differential parity exchange rates calculated in Appendix D. These are used as weights to convert the national income by industrial origin from yuans to rupees. In following this procedure, I have departed substantially from the common practice in China studies, but I have brought it closer to the methodology followed in other comparative studies, most notably those of the USSR.

TABLE 35

Purchasing Parity Rate for Conversion of Yuan into Rupees (Rupee per Yuan)

Sector	Official Rate	Parity Rate
Agriculture	2.00	3.00
Industry	2.00	0.98
Trade, transportation, communication, and finance	2.00	1.70
Other services including government	2.00	2.50

Sources.—Tables D1–D9.

Rate of Growth of National Income

Estimation of China's National Income

Official estimates of national income are presented in table 36. Even this table shows that the rate of growth in parity rupees is more than 17 percent

[63] See Subramanian Swamy, "Retail Price Index in the People's Republic of China," *Review of Economics and Statistics*, vol. 51, no. 3 (August 1969).

[64] *National Income and Capital Formation in Mainland China* (see n. 1 above), p. 12.

lower than the yuan-based rate of growth. However, the official estimates of national income for both China and India cannot be used without some corrections for biases. As already stated, in making these corrections I have essentially followed the methodology of Liu and Yeh. And I have pointed out the differences. Also, I have rather rigorously kept to the U.N. definition of national income, and therefore like Liu and Yeh, I have made significant adjustments in the Chinese definitions of *scope*, *netness*, and *valuation*. As a result, my estimates are closer to what Liu and Yeh call "adjusted Communist estimates" than any other estimates (see table 37).

TABLE 36

OFFICIAL ESTIMATES OF NATIONAL INCOME, CHINA
(1952 PRICES; BILLIONS OF PARITY RUPEES)

Sector	1952	1953	1954	1955	1956	1957	Rates of Growth per Year (%) 1952–57
Agriculture	61.52	62.82	63.99	70.82	72.42	78.32	5.08
Industry	9.79	12.97	15.33	16.41	21.49	24.28	19.13
Construction	1.63	1.95	2.49	2.76	4.48	3.65	20.85
Transport and communication	1.08	1.63	1.61	1.47	1.74	1.74	7.41
Trade	16.42	21.47	21.35	20.86	23.68	20.86	4.28
National income produced	90.44	100.84	104.77	112.32	123.81	128.85	7.22
National income produced (billion yuan)	61.13	70.04	73.88	78.80	89.67	93.53	8.77

SOURCES.—The official data in yuan were taken from Shigeru Ishikawa, "Long-Term Projections of Mainland China's Economy," *Economic Bulletin for Asia and the Far East* (ECAFE), vol. 16, no. 2 (1965); and multiplied by the parity rates in table 35.

Rate of Growth of National Product

The overall rate of growth of national income for the period 1952–65 is about the same in the two countries: 3.0 percent for China, and 3.6 percent for India (table 38). Because of the error involved in national income estimation, the difference cannot be considered significant. Second, it is worth remembering that our estimates are relatively more *favorable* to China than others. The Liu-Yeh estimates (in 1933 prices), for example, yield a significantly lower rate of growth. Third, during the period 1952–65, China's rate of growth declined significantly, whereas India's rate rose.

The rate of growth in China declined from 4.8 percent per year during 1952–59 to 1.4 percent in 1957–65; and during 1961–70 it was still only 1.7 percent per year. On the other hand, the rate of growth in India rose from 3.1 percent during 1952–59 to 4.0 percent during 1957–65 (table 39).

TABLE 37

NET DOMESTIC PRODUCT BY SECTORS, CHINA AND INDIA
(CONSTANT PRICES; BILLIONS OF PARITY RUPEES)

Sector	1952	1953	1954	1955	1956	1957	1958	1959	1960	1961	1962	1963	1964	1965	1970
								China (1952 Prices)							
Agriculture	58.46	60.12	61.08	63.90	66.68	69.10	78.40	72.76	59.00	71.20	73.86	78.99	86.32	87.24	87.98
Industry	17.18	19.50	21.67	23.32	29.59	31.47	40.19	53.37	54.30	38.21	36.75	39.48	42.70	45.96	66.89
Trade, transport, communication, other services	50.34	52.00	54.14	56.11	58.05	59.92	58.40	46.46	32.02	49.15	55.71	61.43	66.01	65.39	45.91
All nonagricultural sectors	67.52	71.50	75.81	79.43	87.64	91.39	98.59	99.83	86.32	87.36	92.46	100.91	108.71	111.35	112.80
Net domestic product	125.98	131.62	136.89	143.33	154.32	160.29	176.99	172.59	145.32	158.56	166.32	179.90	195.03	198.59	200.78
								India (1948–49 Prices)							
Agriculture	44.4	46.0	49.8	50.3	50.2	52.5	50.1	55.6	55.1	59.1	59.1	57.9	59.7	65.1	75.7
Industry	15.2	15.8	16.5	17.0	17.6	18.4	18.6	18.8	19.7	21.1	22.1	23.0	24.4	25.3	30.2
Trade, transport, communication, other services	31.6	32.9	34.0	35.5	37.0	39.0	40.3	42.3	44.1	47.8	50.1	53.0	56.5	60.7	72.5
All nonagricultural sectors combined	46.8	48.7	50.5	52.5	54.6	57.4	58.9	61.1	63.8	68.9	72.2	76.0	80.9	86.0	102.7
Net domestic product	91.2	94.7	100.3	102.8	104.8	109.9	109.0	116.7	118.9	128.0	131.3	133.9	140.6	151.1	178.4

SOURCES.—China: Tables 11, 29, 30, and 33; figures converted by parity rates in table 35. India: *Estimates of National Income and Product*, Conventional Series (New Delhi: Central Statistical Organization, 1971).

TABLE 38
RATE OF GROWTH OF NET DOMESTIC PRODUCT,
CHINA AND INDIA
(% PER YEAR)

Period	China	India
1952–56 to 1957–59	4.8	3.1
1957–59 to 1961–65	1.4	4.0
1961–65 to 1970	1.7	3.8
1952–56 to 1970	2.3	3.7
1952–56 to 1961–65	3.0	3.6

SOURCE.—Table 37.

TABLE 39
RATE OF GROWTH OF PRODUCTION SECTORS, CHINA AND INDIA
(% PER YEAR)

	CHINA			INDIA		
SECTOR	1952–56 to 1957–59	1957–59 to 1961–65	1952–56 to 1961–65	1952–56 to 1957–59	1957–59 to 1961–65	1952–56 to 1961–65
Agriculture	4.2	1.6	2.8	2.3	2.6	2.5
All nonagricultural sectors	6.2	0.5	3.1	3.9	5.2	4.6
Net domestic product	4.8	1.4	3.0	3.1	4.0	3.6

SOURCE.—Table 37.

Based on tentative estimates for 1970, China's rate of growth during the period 1952–70 was 2.3 percent, barely above the rate of growth of population. In India, during the same period, the rate of growth was 3.7 percent per year, much higher than the Chinese rate.

During the decade of the 1950s, China had a significantly higher rate of growth of population. India, on the other hand, was not subjected to such severe disequilibrating shocks[65] and was able not only to maintain the rate of growth but to step up significantly in the second decade.

Rate of Growth of Net Domestic Product by Industrial Origin, China and India, 1952–70

The sectoral rates of growth show some sharp contrasts. While agriculture has performed similarly in both countries over the full period, the rate of agricultural growth is quite sensitive to the choice of terminal year. Thus if we include 1958 in the first period for China, the rate of growth increases substantially. Similarly, if we include 1959–60 in the period 1951–59 for India, its rate of growth also increases. However, our general conclusion regarding the comparative performance is not altered.

The performance of nonagricultural sectors is very different: in China the rate of growth drops from a high of 6.2 percent per year to a low of

[65] India's economy was upset by the Sino-Indian War in 1962, the Indo-Pakistan War in 1965, and a severe drought in 1966 and 1967; but the impact of these disequilibria was not on the scale of those in China.

0.5 percent per year; in India it rises from 3.9 percent per year to 5.2 percent per year. For the period 1952–70 (or 1952–65), as a whole India shows a higher rate of growth of net domestic product than China (3.7 percent vs. 2.3 percent), largely because of a higher rate of growth in the nonagricultural sectors.

Within the nonagricultural sectors, the combined services sector *S* grew at a faster rate in India. While the growth rate of industry during 1952–70 ws 3.8 percent, that of services was 4.7 percent (see tables 32 and 34). In China, the negative rate of growth of services, −1.0 percent, contrasts sharply with the growth rate of industry, 6.8 percent per year. In other words, had the sector not declined, China and India would have experienced the same growth rate in net domestic product. This can be demonstrated easily. Since the shares of A (agriculture), M+ (mining, manufacturing, construction, and utilities), and S (trade and other services) are 44 percent, 25 percent, and 31 percent, respectively, assuming that S grows at the same rate as net domestic product, the Chinese growth rate is $(0.44 \times 0.022) + (0.25 \times 0.068) + (0.31 \times 0.023)$, or 3.4 percent per year, which is close to the Indian growth rate of 3.7 percent per year for the same period.

Sectoral Shares in Net Domestic Product, China and India, 1952–70

The share of agriculture in total product in China and India is typical of less developed countries. In both countries it is more than 40 percent but slightly lower in China than in India (table 40). Further, in both countries it has declined over time: in China from 45.3 percent to 43.8 percent, and in India from 48.8 percent to 42.4 percent. Correspondingly, the share of nonagricultural sectors rose from 54.7 percent to 56.2 percent in China, and from 51.2 percent to 57.6 percent in India. Industrialization, the process of declining shares of agricultural sectors and rising shares of nonagricultural sectors, is observed in the two countries. Within the nonagricultural sectors, the share of the M+ sector rose sharply in China from 16.1 percent in the first period to 33.3 percent in 1970 but hardly changed in India.

TABLE 40

SECTORAL SHARES IN NET DOMESTIC PRODUCT, CHINA AND INDIA

(%)

	A		M+		S		M+ Plus S	
PERIOD	China	India	China	India	China	India	China	India
1952–56	45.3	48.8	16.1	16.6	38.6	34.6	54.7	51.2
1957–59	42.1	47.2	24.6	16.6	33.3	36.2	57.9	52.8
1961–65	44.5	43.9	22.6	16.9	32.9	39.1	55.5	56.1
1970	43.8	42.4	33.3	17.0	22.9	40.6	56.2	57.6

SOURCE.—Table 37.

NOTE.—A = agriculture; M+ = mining, manufacturing, construction, and utilities; S = trade and other services.

The S sector shows a different trend—a decline from 38.6 percent to 22.9 percent in China, and a rise from 34.6 percent to 40.6 percent in India. In other words, while the production structure of agricultural and nonagricultural outputs is about the same in both countries, the subcomponents of the non-A sector are quite different. The Kuznets index of dispersion applied to the shares in table 40 rises from 8.0 in the first period to 35.4 in the second, indicating a sharp difference in sectoral shares over time.

Net Domestic Investment and Incremental Capital-Output Ratio

Estimates of net domestic investment are generally less reliable than other estimates. For China there are two additional complications. First, official estimates are available only for 1952–57. For 1958–65 we have nothing. Second, the Chinese price structure makes it difficult to calculate the capital formation proportion unless one makes rather bold assumptions about the real value of a yuan in investment. To obtain a rough idea of investment in China I have therefore made some unorthodox assumptions. For India the situation is only slightly better, since constant price estimates are not available, and deflation of the current price estimates is arbitrary. Nevertheless, these estimates, although tentative, are shown in table 41.

The rate of investment as a percentage of national income, based on uncorrected Chinese official figures, is high, rising from 18.2 percent in 1952 to 22.5 percent in 1956. Clearly, these rates are overestimates, because a growth rate for this period of 4.8 percent and a rate of investment of around 20 percent would mean an implicit incremental capital-output ratio of 4.2, which is unusually high. Moreover, it is unlikely that capital was used so much more inefficiently in China than in India, where the incremental capital-output ratio was only 2.3.

The Chinese official investment figures indicate two types of bias for which corrections are essential. The first is that of scope,[66] for which the official Chinese definition is narrower than the customarily accepted U.N. definition. Second, as already indicated, the Chinese price system introduces an upward bias into the value of industrial items, including capital formation. We should therefore use differential parity rates for investment and for net domestic product. T. C. Liu has corrected for the first type of bias. For the second type, I converted yuan investment figures to parity rupee figures by multiplying the former by 0.89 (the number of investment yuans per rupee).

If only the price corrections (i.e., second type of bias) are made, the rate of investment for 1952 drops from 18.2 percent to 10.9 percent; for

[66] See K. C. Yeh, "Estimates of Capital Formation in Communist China," in *Economic Trends in Communist China*, ed. Alexander Eckstein, Walter Galenson, and T. C. Liu (Chicago: Aldine Publishing Co., 1968). See also F. M. Cone, *The Rate of Investment and National Product in Communist China*, memoranda RM-5625, 5662, 5841, and 6074-PR/ISA (Santa Monica, Calif.: RAND Corp., 1967).

TABLE 41

RATE OF INVESTMENT, CHINA AND INDIA (ABSOLUTES IN BILLIONS)

Category	1952	1953	1954	1955	1956	1957	1958
	China (1952 Prices)						
Official (yuan):							
1. Accumulation	11.10	15.00	16.50	16.50	18.00	...	...
2. National income produced	61.13	70.04	73.88	78.80	89.67	...	...
3. Rate of investment (lines 1 ÷ 2 × 100)	18.20	21.40	22.30	20.60	22.50	...	...
Official adjusted (yuan):							
4. Net domestic investment	12.07	16.05	17.52	18.40	22.78	18.20	23.60
5. Net domestic product	79.05	81.75	86.35	92.43	103.59	105.81	113.04
6. Rate of investment (lines 4 ÷ 5 × 100)	15.27	19.63	20.29	19.91	21.99	17.20	20.00
Official (parity rupees):							
7. Accumulation	9.88	13.35	14.69	16.02	...	...	...
8. National income produced	90.44	100.84	104.77	112.32	123.81	...	...
9. Rate of investment (lines 7 ÷ 8 × 100)	10.92	13.23	14.02	13.08	12.94	...	...
Official adjusted (parity rupees):							
10. Net domestic investment	10.74	14.28	15.59	16.38	20.27	16.20	21.00
11. Net domestic product	125.98	131.97	137.40	144.18	152.98	159.49	176.99
12. Rate of investment (lines 10 ÷ 11 × 100)............	11.00	14.00	14.80	14.60	16.40	12.90	15.00
	India (1948–49 Prices)						
Official (rupees):							
13. Net domestic investment	7.20	4.17	7.32	8.33	10.38	16.16	12.21
14. Net domestic product.........	91.20	94.70	100.30	102.80	104.80	109.90	109.80
15. Rate of investment (lines 13 ÷ 14 × 100)............	7.90	4.40	7.30	8.10	9.90	14.70	11.20

SOURCES.—Lines 1 and 2: *Ten Great Years* [Wei Dah de Shyr Nian] (Peking: Statistical Publishing House, 1959), p. 20; Lu Guang, "China's National Income," *Peking Review*, no. 6, April 8, 1958. Line 4: T. C. Liu, "Quantitative Trends in the Economy," in *Economic Trends in Communist China*, ed. Alexander Eckstein, Walter Galenson, and T. C. Liu (Chicago: Aldine Publishing Co., 1968). Line 5: Estimates underlying table 37. Lines 7, 8, 10, and 11: Parity conversion is based on rates in table 35. Lines 13 and 14: *Gross Capital Formation* (New Delhi: Central Statistical Organization, 1969). Conversion to constant prices was done by means of a crude capital goods price index which I constructed.

1956 it drops from 22.5 percent to 12.9 percent. The corrected estimates appear more plausible and yield an implicit incremental capital-output of 2.5. Obviously, the Chinese price system needs correction.

Table 42 gives net domestic investment for China and India. The figures for India may be overestimates, since they were deflated by an index

TABLE 42

RATE OF NET DOMESTIC INVESTMENT IN CHINA AND INDIA (PARITY RUPEES)

	CHINA		INDIA	
YEAR	Billion Rupees (1952 Prices) (1)	% NDP (2)	Billion Rupees (1958–59 Prices) (3)	% NDP (4)
1952...........	10.74	8.5	7.20	7.9
1953...........	14.28	10.8	4.17	4.4
1954...........	15.59	11.3	7.32	7.3
1955...........	16.38	11.4	8.33	8.1
1956...........	20.27	13.3	10.38	9.9
1957...........	16.20	10.2	16.16	14.7
1958...........	21.00	11.9	12.21	11.2
1959...........	17.80	10.3	15.52	13.3
1960...........	15.22	10.5	14.51	12.2
1961...........	13.88	8.8	17.79	13.9
1962...........	13.97	8.4	14.57	11.3
1963...........	14.86	8.3	17.94	13.4
1964...........	16.11	8.3	19.68	14.0
1965...........	17.36	8.7	21.60	14.3

SOURCES.—Cols. 1 and 2: 1952–58—Table 41. 1959–65—My estimate. Cols. 3 and 4: 1952–60—Table 41. 1961–65—Estimates are corrected figures in *Estimates of Saving in India* (New Delhi: Central Statistical Organization, 1969), by my rough capital goods price index.

with 1958–59 as base. However, the slight error involved does not affect the comparative performance of the two countries. The rate of investment in China rose from 8.5 percent in 1952 to 13.3 percent in 1956, but declined to 8.8 percent, and never recovered to the pre-Great Leap levels.[67] In India, the rate of investment fluctuated considerably but showed a clear upward trend. Starting from behind China in the early 1950s, the rate of investment began to exceed the Chinese rate in the 1960s. However, in the late 1960s, because of the Drought the rate of investment declined to 8.8 percent in 1970. Very likely, at the start of the 1970s the rate of investment in China and India was about the same: roughly 9 percent of net domestic product.

The figures on the incremental capital-output ratio, derived from table 42, also provide some interesting insights (table 43).

The rate of investment during 1952–59 was higher in China than in India, but the incremental capital-output ratio was lower in China. Hence it may be concluded that the higher rate of growth in China (4.8 percent versus 3.1 percent) is directly related not only to the higher investment rates but also to more efficient use of capital. Not surprisingly, during 1957–65 the rate of investment in China dropped below the Indian rate, and the incremental capital-output ratio rose; as a result the rate of growth of the economy dropped. As a consequence of the trends in the two periods,

[67] The investment ratios are "net domestic" rates. Because of the failure of the Great Leap, the Drought, and the sudden pullout of Russian aid, the "gross national" investment ratios are bound to be higher than the "net domestic" investment ratios.

TABLE 43

RATE OF INVESTMENT AND INCREMENTAL CAPITAL-OUTPUT RATIO, CHINA AND INDIA

PERIOD	CHINA			INDIA		
	Rate of Investment (%) (1)	Rate of Growth (in NDP) (2)	Capital Output Ratio (3)*	Rate of Investment (%) (4)	Rate of Growth (in NDP) (5)	Capital Output Ratio (6)†
1952–59....	11.0	4.8	2.3	9.8	3.1	3.2
1957–65....	9.4	1.4	6.7	13.2	4.0	3.3
1952–65....	10.0	3.0	3.3	11.5	3.6	3.2

SOURCE.—Cols. 1 and 4: Table 42. Cols. 2 and 5: Table 38.
* Cols. 1 ÷ 2.
† Cols. 4 ÷ 5.

the picture for 1952–65 is similar to that for India: the rate of investment, the rate of growth, and the incremental capital-output ratio are about the same in both countries—around 11 percent, 3.0 and 3.6 percent, and 3.2 percent, respectively.

Appendix D
Calculation of the Sectoral Parity Price Ratio between Yuan and Rupee

Parity price ratios, namely, yuan divided by rupee, have been calculated at the wholesale, retail, and foreign trade levels, and discussion is organized in this sequence.

I rely primarily on two sources, neither of which has yet been translated. The first is *Industrial Equipment and Materials*[68] which gives considerable information on producer goods prices. The prices refer to December 1, 1951 or thereabouts, but they are close to wholesale prices prevailing in the third quarter of 1952, the base of the calculation of Chinese national product estimates. Prices did rise after December 1, 1951, but since most of the rise was in producer goods our findings would be strengthened if the "third quarter of 1952" prices were used.

The second source is *Shin Chugoku Keizai no Bunseki: Bukka Hen* [An analysis of China's economy], which mainly gives retail prices of many commodities observed by Japanese travelers in eight or nine cities from 1953 to 1960. Although travelers' reports are not the most reliable, I have used them and find that they yield some interesting results. Since I have not been able to assemble the wholesale prices for 1957 systematically, I used the 1956–57 retail prices to calculate parity rates between the yuan and the rupee. These two basic sources have been supplemented with Chinese newspaper quotations of various prices, cross-checked with other material.

Wholesale Prices: Rupee-Yuan Ratios

Comparison is based on price availability for China, and 198 commodities have been compared. The Chinese prices, f.o.b. factory or warehouse as of

[68] Nos. 77–78, January 10, 1952, published by the Ministry of Heavy Industry, People's Republic of China. Data are also presented in yuan-dollar ratios by Chao Kang, "Two Studies on Mainland China's Economy," Occasional Paper no. 2, Center for Chinese Studies, University of Michigan, 1963.

December 1951, have been obtained from two sources: (1) producer goods prices mostly from *Industrial Equipment and Materials*, and (2) newspaper quotations. ("1952 prices" refer to the third quarter of 1952. Indian data are from the Economic Adviser's Office, Ministry of Commerce, New Delhi.)

One major problem in the comparison is the inadequate description of commodities. In many cases, as Kang notes,[69] comparability is not difficult: (1) chemicals (by purity), (2) timber and metal products (by size), (3) cotton yarn (by count), (4) machinery (by h.p. or kwh). In groups such as meat, vegetable oils, steel, nonferrous metals, ingots, building materials, because of homogeneity the error cannot be large. For the remaining commodities, such as pens, bicycles, and cigarettes, ad hoc methods have to be used.

Chinese weights were used. Theoretical discussion necessarily relates to the index number problems. Two lessons can be drawn from this: (1) The true difference between India and China is better approximated in Indian prices. (2) The rates of growth when calculated with Indian weights are relatively more accurate, on the crucial assumption of *Gerschenkron Effect.*

Another supporting argument can be advanced for this conclusion. Just as it has been argued that in time-series comparisons prices for the most recent year should be used, we can argue that, in comparing China and India, India's prices should be used—since the Chinese outputs are being looked at from the Indian vantage point. If one looked at India from the Chinese vantage point, although the opposite conclusion might be reached, it is unlikely because the economies of China and India are not too dissimilar. Conclusions on relative performance would be the same, regardless of vantage point. The absolute rates of growth are higher for both China and India when evaluated in Chinese prices rather than Indian prices.

To calculate the purchasing power parity rate by sectors based on wholesale prices, a two-step procedure is adopted. First, the relative price ratio, p_i/p_c, for 198 commodities is calculated. Second, the yuan value, $p_c q_c$, is multiplied by p_i/p_c to obtain the value of Chinese production in rupees. The first step also yields the purchasing power parity rate of exchange between yuan and rupee. For expository ease, the results presented in tables D1 and D2 are summarized in two ways: (1) in subcategories—I, commodities related primarily to consumption (63 items); II, fuels and electricity (8 items); III, commodities related primarily to production as intermediate inputs (115 items); IV, machinery (12 items); and (2) in a probability distribution of price ratios, that is, in the form of a histogram.

Four observations may be derived from table D1: (1) The rupee per yuan, yuan per dollar parity rates diverge from the official exchange rates. (2) The divergence differs significantly among the categories of commodities, and the deviation from the exchange rate is greatest for fuels and electricity and least for consumption goods. (3) Machinery is more expensive in China than one would expect from the exchange rate conversion. This is not surprising because, as Chinese economists maintain, high machinery prices bring in good budget revenue.[70] (4) The implied rupee per dollar rate bears out the expectations that primary goods are cheaper in India while producer goods are more expensive than the exchange rate would indicate. However, overall exchange rate is close to the parity rate.

The frequency distribution of price relatives yields further findings on the parity rate (table D2). Since our aim is to demonstrate the variability in

[69] Chao Kang, *The Rate of Pattern of Industrial Growth in Communist China* (see n. 32 above).

[70] Nan Ping and So Chen, "The Prices of the Means of Production," *Jing Jih Yan Jiou*, no. 2 (1957), pp. 17–18.

parity rates, the frequency intervals are in number of yuans per dollar instead of number of yuans per rupee. The median and modal price ratios are greater than the exchange rate of $1.00 = 2.46¥, indicating that the distribution is skewed away from the official exchange rate. Second, the distribution is most concentrated for consumption goods and least concentrated for producer goods or "all commodities" combined. This finding lends support to our earlier conclusion that industrial goods in China are more overpriced than agricultural goods. Hence, using the exchange rate for converting yuans to other currencies introduces a bias in national estimation: a higher weight is assigned to a faster growing sector, causing an upward bias in the rate of growth of the Chinese national income.

Mah Feng-hwa has raised an objection to this type of comparison.[71] He suggests that, in order to get a more correct idea of exchange rate, only goods that enter into international trade transactions should be compared. However, even his calculations, shown in tables D3 and D4, strengthen the above conclusion because the parity rate works out to $1.00 = 5.42¥. Furthermore, the more the commodity being compared is processed, or produced with a higher capital-labor ratio, the greater the overvaluation of the yuan. This is further proof that the yuan is not only overvalued but is more overvalued with respect to industrial goods. Another approach is to observe the parity rate for China's *exports*—mostly agricultural—which works out to $1.00 = 3.37¥. The parity rate of China's imports—mostly industrial goods—works out to $1.00 = 7.82¥.

Another objection may be raised at this juncture. Since India and the United States are noncontrolled economies and their trade with China is negligible, it could be argued that such a price comparison is not appropriate. In order to meet this criticism, I calculated the price parity between China and Japan. The comparison of wholesale prices is shown in table D5, which reveals similar results to those obtained earlier. For most commodities the yuan is overvalued, and the more processed the product, the greater the overvaluation. The picture is basically the same in 1952 as in 1957, with one important difference: the industrial product overvaluation is less in 1957.

Comparison of Chinese Domestic Price with Export Price

The Chinese appear to have two main reasons for exporting: (1) to earn foreign exchange to pay for machinery imports needed for economic growth, and (2) to facilitate economic assistance to friendly countries. Trade is thus based neither on international division of labor considerations nor on any other variation of the comparative advantage logic. Therefore, the currently used exchange rate, $1.00 = 2.3¥, is not an equilibrium or quasi-equilibrium rate that equates the demand and supply of traded goods. In order to observe the difference between domestic and export prices, international trade data are examined. For China, more data on international trade are available than on domestic trade goods because they appear in the publications of her trading partner countries. Only China's trade with two of her major partners, Japan and Hong Kong, is considered. The evidence is summarized in tables D6, D7, and D8.

The following conclusions are based on the evidence in these tables. First, if the dollar/yuan ratio exceeded 0.424 (the official exchange rate), it implies that the yuan is *undervalued*, that is, the Chinese earn a larger number of yuan per ton from foreign trade than from domestic trade in the same commodity. Similarly, if the dollar/yuan ratio is less than 0.424, the Chinese

[71] *The Foreign Trade of Communist China* (Chicago: Aldine Publishing Co., 1971).

are suffering a net "loss" from international trade, because yuans earned are less from foreign than from internal trade, and the yuan is overvalued in primary foodstuffs, which were by no means in abundant supply in China. In fact, for most of the period from 1950 to 1966, these commodities were rationed. Obviously, the official exchange rate does not reflect the social opportunity cost of these commodities. Third, the trade in salt, coal, pig iron, cotton cloth, caustic soda, carbonic soda, and cement, that is, in non-foodstuffs, was a net loss to China.[72] Thus China did not have a competitive position in those commodities at the official exchange rate of $1.00 = 0.424¥. Fourth, table D8 shows the special feature of Chinese domestic price formation: while it is uncompetitive and not beneficial to trade in nonfoodstuffs when the calculation is made in wholesale prices, in *transfer prices* the trade is profitable. This means that the profit and tax components which account for the difference between transfer and wholesale prices are a major factor in the Chinese price structure. The complication is that the nonfood items in China are overvalued. Findings based on wholesale and retail prices are thus confirmed by the results based on transfer prices.

Rupee-Yuan Parity Ratios on the Basis of Retail Prices

Data on retail prices have been collected from *Shin Chugoku Keizai no Bunseki*, other visitor reports, and newspaper reports. For the purpose of comparison, 1955–58 has been chosen as the base period for two reasons. First, these 4 years appear to be good years in both countries. In India the price decline of 1952–54 had been arrested and had given way to rising retail prices. This price element may bias the result in favor of a higher parity rate between the yuan and the rupee, but, if it does, the effect is not substantial. China had also raised retail prices in 1957, although many economists in China held that the rise was inadequate. Second, since we are concerned here with the question of valuation, the structure of prices around the year 1957 is important, since 1957 may be considered an alternative base year.

The question of reliability of the Japanese traveler data is now considered. These are, of course, subject to the usual sampling and especially nonsampling errors, such as recall lapse and copying errors. On these grounds certain price quotations were rejected. For instance, for most commodities and for most years, prices were available regionally for several cities. For some commodities, two or more price quotations were available for the same cities. In all such cases, if the mean retail price as a ratio of the price *range* exceeded unity, the price quotations were rejected. It can be easily shown by means of the Tchebyscheff lemma and the mathematical relation between range and variance that the error is not more than 10 percent under such a procedure. The Japanese price data come out reasonably well in this test.

Table D9 suggests the following conclusions. First, the exchange rate overvalues the yuan. Second, luxuries and subsidiary foods appear to be undervalued in China, but this is a reflection of the high price of luxuries and subsidiary foods in India due to the inequality of income and the tax evasion in India. The unaccounted or tax-evaded incomes in India generally purchase

[72] When we compare the official exchange rate of the people's yuan to the U.S. dollar (0.424) with the purchasing power ratio of the people's yuan and the U.S. dollar or exported goods, we can say that agricultural goods are traded at a relatively more advantageous price than industrial goods. As mentioned before, however, there is a large difference for the same commodity between the wholesale price of the National Commercial Agency and the transfer price (in the agricultural goods) assigned directly to the enterprise. This price difference can range from 50 to 150 percent.

high Engel elasticity goods, since such incomes can only be used for consumption goods if they are to escape detection. Third, the relative price of consumer durable goods in China vis-à-vis India is far above the exchange rate of 0.50 yuan to the rupee. This is in general accord with the Chinese policy of pricing products proportional to the average cost and allowing for a tax and profit margin at a higher rate for more capital-intensive goods. Fourth, the overall parity rates show that the Chinese yuan is overvalued, and more so for processed goods; the rate implied for Japan vis-à-vis India corresponds roughly to the exchange rate between Japanese yen and rupees, lending further evidence to the finding that the Chinese yuan is overvalued.

Thus, the analysis of retail prices lends support to the findings that the yuan is overvalued and that the industrial sectors need differential parity rates for conversion of yuan into rupees.

TABLE D1

WEIGHTED RUPEE-YUAN-DOLLAR PRICE RATIOS (WHOLESALE PRICES)

		WEIGHTED PRICE RATIOS		
CATEGORY	No. PRICE RATIOS	Rs./¥ Using Chinese Weights	¥/$ Using U.S. Weights	Rs./$ Gross Rate
Commodities related primarily to consumption .	63	1.70	2.46	4.18
Fuels and electricity......	8	0.44	9.81	4.31
Intermediate inputs	115	0.89	8.33	7.41
Machinery..............	12	0.77	9.00	7.20
All commodities.......	198	1.52	4.13	4.68
Official exchange rates..	...	2.00	2.43	4.76

SOURCES.—Rs./¥ figures, see text. Basic data: *Gong Yeh Ji Tsair*, January 10, 1952; T. C. Liu and K. C. Yeh, *The Economy of Mainland China* (Princeton, N.J.: Princeton University Press, 1965). India: *Wholesale Prices* (New Delhi: Economic Adviser, Ministry of Commerce and Industry, 1953). Subramanian Swamy, *Handbook of Commercial Information*, (New Delhi: Ministry of Commerce and Industry, 1963); Chao Kang, "Two Studies on Mainland China's Economy," Occasional Paper no. 2, Center for Chinese Studies, University of Michigan, 1963; and Chao Kang, *The Rate and Pattern of Industrial Growth in Communist China* (Ann Arbor: University of Michigan Press, 1965).

TABLE D2

FREQUENCY DISTRIBUTION OF PRICE RELATIVES, 1951
(YUANS PER DOLLAR)

PRICE RATIO (¥/$)	NO. COMMODITIES BY CATEGORY				
	I	II	III	IV	Total
0–3	37	0	11	0	48
4–6	18	5	21	1	45
7–9	5	0	27	8	40
10–12	2	0	18	1	21
13–15	1	0	12	2	15
16–18	0	0	12	0	12
19–21	0	0	3	0	3
22–24	0	0	2	0	2
25–27	0	0	5	0	5
Above 27	0	3	4	0	7
Total	63	8	115	12	198

TABLE D3

CHINESE-AMERICAN DOMESTIC PRICE RATIOS OF COMMUNIST CHINA'S IMPORTS FROM THE FREE WORLD

Commodity	1951 Value Weight (%)	Average Price Ratio (¥/$)	No. Prices Compared
Fish	0.05	9.20	2
Food, beverage, and tobacco (except fish and dairy products)	1.40	3.20	15
Oilseeds, fats, and oils	0.31	1.92	7
Crude rubber	27.16	7.04	11
Wood, cork, and manufactures (except paper)	0.31	2.85	9
Paper, paperboard, and manufactures	4.85	11.00	3
Raw wool	0.51	3.06	1
Raw cotton	12.18	1.95	1
Other textile fibers and manufactures	11.57	3.36	21
Other inedible crude materials and manufactures	0.95	5.19	10
Fertilizers, crude, and manufactures	3.06	8.39	4
Nonmetallic minerals and manufactures	1.26	22.78	8
Iron, steel, and manufactures	11.81	11.70	31
Base metal ores, base metals, and manufactures	1.43	10.23	14
Dyeing, tanning, and coloring materials	8.11	11.09	4
Medicines and pharmaceuticals	8.00	6.55	6
Other chemicals	7.04	15.10	22
Total	100.00	7.82	169

SOURCES.—See text and relevant footnotes. The average and weighted price ratios are all computed by Mah Feng-hwa, *The Foreign Trade of Communist China* (Chicago: Aldine Publishing Company, 1971).

TABLE D4

CHINESE-AMERICAN DOMESTIC PRICE RATIOS OF COMMUNIST CHINA'S EXPORTS TO THE FREE WORLD

Commodity	1951 Value Weight (%)	Average Price Ratio (¥/$)	No. Prices Compared
Live animals and meat	3.21	1.50	7
Cereals and preparations	6.71	2.36	5
Fruits and vegetables	8.02	3.34	5
Sugar	0.89	8.14	1
Other food, beverage, and tobacco	12.60	2.20	6
Oilseeds	25.49	1.08	2
Oils and fats	10.81	2.22	6
Wood and lumber, unmanufactured	0.01	2.57	8
Other wood, paper, and manufactures	1.99	9.53	4
Wool and manufactures	2.81	4.56	5
Cotton and manufactures	4.20	3.02	15
Other textile fibers and manufactures	7.62	2.65	3
Parskins and manufactures	0.45	4.34	4
Other inedible crude materials and manufactures	9.66	6.97	11
Fertilizers, crude, and manufactures	0.02	8.39	4
Coal and related fuels	0.05	3.46	3
Basemetals, ores, and manufactures	0.96	9.60	17
Chemicals (except fertilizers)	4.71	13.10	32
Total	100.00	3.37	138

SOURCES.—Same as table D3.

TABLE D5

COMPARATIVE PRICE LEVEL, CHINA AND JAPAN (WHOLESALE)

Commodity	1952	1957
Textile material	0.52	1.01
Fuels	0.94	0.79
Metal and its products	4.06	2.24
Building materials	1.44	1.23
Chemical products	1.38	2.41
Miscellaneous producer goods	1.22	2.63
Agriculture production for food	0.53	0.54
Other food	1.05	1.17
Textile products	2.20	3.35
Miscellaneous consumer goods	2.07	1.96
Miscellaneous durable consumer goods	4.06	2.24
Official exchange rate (yen/yuan)	150	150

SOURCE.—Shigeru Ishikawa, "Stragegy of Foreign Trade—with Special Reference to China," *Hitotsubashi Journal of Economics* (January 1965).

NOTES.—The price ratio, $p_c \div p_j$, is divided by the going exchange rate of 1 yuan = 0.006836 yen. Thus, if any item exceeds unity, that item is overvalued in China vis-à-vis Japan.

TABLE D6

COMPARISON BETWEEN SHANGHAI WHOLESALE PRICE AND EXPORT PRICE TO JAPAN
(FOB DOLLAR PER TON)

COMMODITY	1957 SHANGHAI WHOLESALE PRICES PEOPLE'S (¥/TON) (1)	EXPORT PRICES TO JAPAN ($/TON) 1957 (2)	1963 (3)	1964 (4)	1965 (5)	1966 (6)	$/PEOPLE'S ¥ 2 ÷ 1	3 ÷ 1	4 ÷ 1	5 ÷ 1	6 ÷ 1
Rice:											
Nonglutenized	...	...	...	...	154.7	161.7	...	...	...	0.51	0.53
Polished	303	...	...	...	156.1	154	...	...	...	0.52	0.51
Soybeans, medium quality	215	109.6	103.7	110.6	118.3	131.6	0.51	0.49	0.51	0.55	0.61
Hwaipei salt	246	5.3	5.4	5.6	5.7	5.7	0.02	0.02	0.02	0.02	0.02
China wood oil	1,276	532	798–806	747–714	423–574	423	0.42	0.63	0.45–0.56	0.33–0.45	0.33
Iron ore	...	...	...	6.8	7.9	7.0	...	...	...	...	...
Smokeless coal	32.1	12.6	...	11.7	11.2	11.0	0.39	...	0.36	0.36	0.34
Coal for coke	33	10.3	10.1	10.1	10.2	10.1	0.31	0.31	0.31	0.31	0.31
Pig iron, no. 2 national produce	220	98	37.8	40.6	41.5	38.7	0.45	0.17	0.18	0.18	0.18

SOURCES.—Shanghai wholesale price: *Price statistics of Commodities in Pre and Past Liberation of Shanghai* (Shanghai: Shanghai People's Publishing House, 1958). Export prices to Japan: *Statistics on Import Permission* (Tokyo: Ministry of Commerce, 1958). Table is from Shigeru Ishikawa. *Long-Term View of the Chinese Economy* (Tokyo: Institute of Asian Economic Affairs, 1965), vol. 2.

NOTES.—Export prices to Japan are FOB prices, except for the price of China wood oil which is CIF price; the distinction between CIF and FOB is not clear for 1957. Official rate between the People's ¥ and the U.S. $ is 0.424 (U.S. $/People's ¥). Big changes are seen for China wood oil, depending upon quality.

TABLE D7

COMPARISON BETWEEN SHANGHAI WHOLESALE PRICE AND EXPORT PRICE TO HONG KONG

(CIF DOLLAR PER TON)

COMMODITY	1956 SHANGHAI WHOLESALE PRICE (¥/TON) (1)	EXPORT PRICE TO HONG KONG ($) 1956 (2)	1965 (3)	$/¥ 2 ÷ 1	3 ÷ 1
Rice, nonglutinous rice average..	272	137	148.6	0.50	0.55
Wheat, medium quality.........	199	115		0.58	...
Soybeans, medium quality	215	118	115.5	0.55	0.54
Sugar	1,254	112	86.6	0.09	0.87
Pork, good quality.............	1,340	754	463.6	0.56	0.35
Eggs..........................	1,044	706	...	0.68	...
Hwaipei salt	213	10	7.8	0.05	0.04
China wood oil................	1,090	471	465.5	0.43	0.43
Iron ore.......................	...	...	5.0	...	...
Smokeless coal................	32.1	...	13.8	...	0.43
Pig iron, no. 2 national produce .	220	...	49.7	...	0.23
Cotton cloth, 12 lb.	694	150	...	0.22	...
Caustic soda, Biri product	956	80	89.8	0.08	0.09
Carbonic soda	640	48	...	0.08	...
Cement, Raishan brand	73	19	15.5	0.26	0.21

SOURCES.—For Shanghai price: see table D6 (cf. table 7 in that source). For Hong Kong price: Ajia Keizai Kenkyu-shu, ed., *Statistical Study of Chinese Economic Development*, vol. 3 (Tokyo: Institute for Asian Economic Affairs, 1967); *Hong Kong Trade Statistics for 1965* (Hong Kong: Government of Hong Kong, 1966).

TABLE D8

COMPARISON BETWEEN PURCHASE PRICE OR TRANSFER PRICE AND EXPORT PRICE TO JAPAN

Commodity	1957 Shanghai Wholesale Price (¥/Ton) (1)	Purchase Price Transfer Price (¥/Ton) (2)	Export Prices to Japan ($/Ton)			$/¥		
			1957 (3)	1965 (4)	July 1966 (5)	3 ÷ 2	4 ÷ 2	5 ÷ 2
Rice, nonglutinous polished	303	252–273	. . .	154.7	161.7	. . .	0.61–0.56	0.64–0.58
Soybeans, medium quality	215	197	109.6	118.3	131.6	0.56	0.60	0.67
Hwaipei salt, salt tax deducted	246	106	5.3	5.7	5.7	0.06	0.06	0.05
China wood oil	1,276	. . .	532.0	423.0–574.0	423.0	0.42	0.33–0.45	0.33
Smokeless coal	32.1	12.7	12.6	11.2	11.0	0.99	0.88	0.87
Coke coal	33	12.7	10.3	10.2	10.1	0.81	0.80	0.80
Pig iron no. 2 national produce	220	152 (75)	98.0	41.5	38.7	0.64 (1.31)	0.27 (0.55)	0.25 (0.52)

SOURCES.—Soybeans and rice: *The China Study Monthly*, no. 163 (1967). Salt: 140 ¥/ton for salt tax is deducted from wholesale price. Coal: Ajia Keizai Kenkyu-shu, *Study of Economy* (Tokyo: Institute of Asian Economic Affairs, 1957). Pig iron: Shigeru Ishikawa, *Statistical Study of Chinese Economic Development*, no. 102 (Tokyo: Institute of Asian Economic Affairs, 1965), but figures in parentheses are original price at factory in Anchan.

TABLE D9

Parity Comparison, China, India, and Japan, 1953–58
(Retail Prices)

Commodity	Official Exchange Rate: Chinese ¥ to Rs. (Rs./¥)	Official Exchange Rate: Chinese ¥ to Yen (Yen/¥)	Relative Price Ratio: Indian and Chinese (Rs./¥)	Relative Price Ratio: Japanese and Chinese (Yen/¥)
Food	2.00	150	1.70	148
Subsidiary food	2.00	150	2.73	263
Special luxuries	2.00	150	2.23	121
Clothing	2.00	150	0.97	59
Fuel	2.00	150	1.34	556
Daily necessaries	2.00	150	0.89	63
Consumer durables	2.00	150	1.08	81
Cultural	2.00	150	1.35	248
Total	2.00	150	1.61	129

Sources.—Primarily based on *Shin Chogaku no Bunseki* (Tokyo: Tao Keisai Kenkyu Kai, 1961), pp. 97–153. The exchange rate is, however, from an official Chinese publication, *Shyh Shyr Shoou Tseh*, no. 3 (February 1965), pp. 37–38. The numbers are a result of weighting according to the consumer budget in Shanghai (1956), given in Chen Nai-ruenn, *Economic Statistics of the Chinese Mainland* (Chicago: Aldine Publishing Co., 1967).

Appendix E
A Comparison of the Estimated Growth Rate with Alternative Estimates, China

It cannot be overemphasized that the output figures for China which are used here are relatively the most favorable. If I had used the Western scholars' estimates for China, I would have obtained a significantly lower rate of growth. The estimates for India that I have used have been widely accepted by scholars, but even these have been adjusted here and elsewhere.[73]

Only Liu and Yeh, besides myself, have attempted to calculate the rate of growth of China for the period 1952–65. Although the Liu-Yeh rate, 3.8 percent per year,[74] is higher than my estimate of 3.0 percent, it is quite close to the nonmoving average compound rate of 3.6 percent. Also, according to Liu and Yeh, the rate of growth dropped sharply. It would seem that their and my rates are not based on the same premises, since rates for subperiods differ substantially. I feel that the Liu-Yeh rate of growth for 1952–57 is an overestimate, since the special features of the Chinese price system were not taken into account. Moreover, in an illustrative calculation using 1933 prices, they get a lower rate of growth, 4.4 percent, which is close to my estimate of 4.8 percent. This alone should alert us to the peculiarities of the Chinese price system, *since in most cases the further back the price base is shifted, the larger the calculated rate of growth.* This phenomenon is recognized as the Gerschenkron Price Effect. The Chinese experience contradicts the Gerschenkron Law,

[73] Subramanian Swamy, "Economic Growth and the Size Distribution of Income: The Case of India," *Review of Income and Wealth*, vol. 2 (June 1967).

[74] It is not clear how they calculated the rate of growth. It appears that they have used a nonmoving average year-to-year compound rate. Hence, for comparison, I have especially derived the year rate for 1952–65.

implying some peculiar feature in the price system.[75] The Liu-Yeh estimates for 1956–65 are too low because their agricultural production figure is a serious underestimate.[76]

For 1957–65 my estimate of 3.0 percent per year agrees well with Perkins's estimate of 3.1–3.4 percent but is considerably higher than the Field-interpolated estimates of 2.0–2.3 percent. Briefly, my estimate of 3.0 percent per year for 1952–65 cannot be considered as an underestimate compared with the estimates of other China scholars (table E1).

The official estimate of the growth rate is, of course, significantly higher: 8.8 percent during 1952–57, and 5.6 percent during 1957–70. But since these estimates are based on gross value-added and exclude the slowly growing services sector, the growth rate is highly overestimated and cannot be accepted.

TABLE E1

GROWTH RATE OF TOTAL PRODUCT ACCORDING TO VARIOUS SCHOLARS, CHINA (% PER YEAR)

Source	1952–57	1957–65	1957–70	1952–65
1. Liu-Yeh (1952 prices)	6.2	1.6	n.e.	3.8
2. Liu-Yeh (1933 prices)	4.4	n.e.	n.e.	n.e.
3. Perkins	n.e.	3.1–3.4	n.e.	n.e.
4. Field projected	n.e.	2.0–2.3	n.e.	n.e.
5. Official Chinese	8.8	n.e.	5.6	n.e.
6. Swamy	4.8*	3.0*	2.3**	3.6* (3.0)**

SOURCES.—Line 1: T. C. Liu and K. C. Yeh, *The Economy of the Chinese Mainland* (Princeton, N.J.: Princeton University Press, 1965), p. 120. Line 2: W. W. Hollister, *China's Gross National Product and Social Accounts* (Glencoe, Ill.: Free Press, 1959). Line 3: D. H. Perkins, "Economic Growth and the Cultural Revolution," *China Quarterly*, no. 29 (January-March 1967). Line 4: Perkins, p. 9. Line 5: 1952–57 —*Ten Great Years* [Wei Dah de Shyr Nian] (Peking: Statistical Publishing House, 1959). 1957–70—Chou En-lai's interview with Edgar Snow, *Epoca*, February 28, 1971. Line 6: Table 38.

NOTE.—n.e. = not estimated.

* Calculated as a compound rate based on 2 years: 1952 and 1957, and 1957 and 1965.

** Based on moving averages.

TABLE E2

BREAKDOWN OF ADJUSTMENTS MADE IN OFFICIAL RATE OF GROWTH, 1952–57 (% PER YEAR)

Category	Adjustment	Corrected Rate
Official Chinese rate	...	8.80
Adjustments in agricultural production	1.05	7.75
Adjustments in consumer goods production	0.31	7.44
Interaction effects	1.10	6.34
Use of parity prices	1.54	4.80

SOURCE.—The figures in the table were derived by the use of simple identities.

[75] Furthermore, the 1933 prices in China are more likely to reflect factor scarcities and marginal utilities than the 1952 prices.

[76] For a criticism, see Dwight H. Perkins, "Comments on Professor Ta-chung Liu's Paper" (paper read at University of Chicago Conference on China's Heritage and the Communist Political System, 1967).

However, Chou En-lai's figures indicate one important finding that supports our earlier conclusion: during the 1960s the rate of economic progress declined.

Since our estimate (4.8 percent for 1952–57) differs widely from the official rate (8.8 percent per year), we give the breakdown of the differences between the two (table E2).

V. Summary of Findings

National income and its sectoral components are basic data for the analysis and evaluation of economic growth. We have found that these basic data for both China and India suffer from biases of scope, valuation, and comparability. Hence, as a first step it was necessary to reshape and recalculate the national accounts data for both countries to achieve some comparability of concept before a quantitative analysis of growth performance could be attempted. This recalculation was done at the level of the major industrial origins (e.g., agriculture, industry, and services) of national product. On the basis of this revaluation, the following findings were suggested.

1. During 1952–65, foodgrains output (after removing the husk and including potatoes in grain equivalents) grew 3.0 percent per year in India and 2.6 percent per year in China. When the time period was extended to include 1966–70, the Chinese foodgrains growth rate dropped (perhaps because of the Cultural Revolution) to 2.2. percent per year and that of India also dropped to 2.9 percent per year. During the first decade, namely, 1952–59, the Chinese foodgrains growth rate was 4.3 percent per year, substantially higher than the Indian growth rate of 2.7 percent per year. In the subsequent decade, the Chinese growth rate fell to 1.4 percent per year, while the growth rate in India rose to 3.2 percent.

2. The absolute level of output of foodgrains was higher in China than in India during the entire period. The average ratio of output in China to that in India was 2.0, but it was higher in the first decade and lower in the second. The main reason for the difference in absolute outputs is the yield per hectare.

3. For nonfoodgrain crops, the Indian performance was better. The growth rate during 1952–65 was 2.9 percent per year in India and −2.3 percent per year in China.

4. Value-added in agriculture during 1952–70 grew 2.9 percent in India and 2.2 percent in China. However, during 1952–65, the growth rate of net value-added in agriculture was 2.8 percent per year in China versus 2.5 percent in India. During the 1960s, the rate of growth of value-added in agriculture in China was only 1.4 percent whereas that in India was 3.3 percent. Consequently, the growth rate in net value-added in agriculture was higher in India than China during the fall period 1952–70.

The years 1952–70 form a period of significant "ups and downs" for Chinese agriculture. During the 1950s the rate of growth of net value-added in agriculture in China was high—4.2 percent per year. Then it dropped sharply during 1958–63 to 1.6 percent per year and rose again to a high of 5 percent during 1963–65, but it declined again to 0 percent during 1965–70. In India, while there were some cyclic movements on a year-to-year basis, the trend rate is steadily upward for 2.3 percent in the 1950s, to 2.6 percent during 1958–63, to 3.3 percent during 1963–70.

5. The rate of growth of industrial production was about the same in China and India: during 1952–65 around 7.0 percent per year. When the period was extended to 1970, the rate dropped for both China and India, but the drop in the Indian rate was much greater. Hence, the average rate of growth of industrial production during 1952–70 was 6.7 percent in China and 6.1 percent in India.

During the subperiod 1952–59, China's growth rate was very high, 17.6 percent per year, compared with 6.6 percent in India. However, thereafter the Chinese rate declined sharply to −1.6 percent, whereas in India the growth rate accelerated from 6.6 percent to 7.4 percent per year.

6. The rates of growth of the petroleum, ferrous metals, and chemical products industries in China exceeded 20 percent during the first decade. Those for the textile and food industries were low, as might have been expected. In India, electric power, construction, petroleum, and metal products performed better than other industries.

7. Although during 1953–70 the rates of growth of factory industrial output were similar—6.7 and 6.1 percent, respectively—that for net value-added in industry (which also includes small industries and handicraft outputs, construction, mining, trade, transport, and communication) was much higher in China than in India—6.8 and 3.8 percent per year, respectively.

8. The trend in net value-added in industry in China reflects the trend in factory output. Thus, during 1952–59, the rate of growth of China's net value-added in industry was 15.4 percent per year, that of factory output was 17.6 percent; during 1958–65 it decreased to −0.3 percent and −1.6 percent, respectively; and in 1963–70 it increased to 7.1 percent and 6.1 percent per year, respectively. In India, because the weight of factory output is smaller, its trend is not reflected in the trend in net value-added in industry. Thus, although factory output grew 6.6 percent to 7.4 percent per year during 1952–65, net value-added increased only 3.1 percent to 4.4 percent. Furthermore, although the growth rate of factory output declined sharply from 7.1 percent for 1952–65 to 4.0 percent for 1962–70, the rate for net value-added remained constant at 3.8 percent.

9. The rates of growth of net domestic product were quite similar in China and India during 1952–65 (3.6 percent in India and 3.0 percent in China). However, if the period is extended to 1970, they are significantly different (3.7 percent in India and 2.3 percent in China).

10. The rate of growth of net domestic product by subperiods showed a significant deceleration in China: from 4.8 percent during 1952–59 to 1.4 percent per year during 1957–65. Although the growth rate accelerated slightly thereafter to 1.7 percent per year, the peak rates of the 1950s were never regained.

In India, growth rate grew steadily from 3.1 percent to 4.0 percent per year during 1952–65, although during 1965–70 it declined slightly to 3.8 percent.

11. The broad conclusion that we can reach is that (*a*) the growth rate of the Chinese and Indian economies has been about the same over the period 1952–70, and (*b*) there has been a significant deceleration in growth rates in China, especially during 1952–65, and a significant acceleration in India.

12. The rate of investment, the ratio to net domestic product in China during 1952–65, was 10 percent, and in India 11.5 percent. But in 1952–59 it was 11.0 percent in China and 9.8 percent in India. The implied incremental capital-output ratio was 3.2–3.3 for both countries during 1952–65. However, while it was more or less unchanged in India during the subperiods, in China the incremental capital-output ratio rose from 2.3 to 6.7 in the 1960s.

Note Added in Proof.—The trickle of data available for 1971 and 1972 lend support to the above conclusions. For example, official Chinese sources place *unhusked* grain output at 246 and 237 million metric tons for the two years. In the same period, India's output of grain was 107 and 104 million metric tons. The U.N. estimate of 10 percent growth rate of the Chinese economy was based on the Chinese official data on gross value of production, and not on net value-added. Therefore, it does not indicate the true position.

Acknowledgments

This work is a product of research conducted while at Harvard University and subsequently at Indian Institute of Technology, Delhi. In my research I have benefited very considerably from the advice of a number of eminent scholars, but the most profound influence has been that of Professor Simon Kuznets with whom I started working on quantitative economics in 1962. It is impossible for me to thank him adequately; I hope he finds this work at least a small reward for being my *guru* for nearly a decade.

When I began research for this work, I came into contact with Professor Shigeru Ishikawa of Hitotsubashi University. Professor Ishikawa was most generous with his time, so that I was properly initiated into the intricacies involved in the study of the economy of China. Through correspondence and my visits to Japan and his indulgence I was able to obtain a considerable amount of material without which the study could not have been possible. Professor Dwight Perkins of Harvard University encouraged me greatly, read my drafts with patience, made penetrating observations on the drafts, and took keen interest in the results of my work.

I should also like to thank Professor John Fairbank, Professor Henry Rosovsky, and Professor Walter Galenson for comments, criticisms, and for assistance in obtaining financial funds through Harvard University and the Committee on the Economy of China.

Mrs. Penny Gustafson very patiently typed several drafts of this work. My apologies and thanks to her. Mrs. Lilian Weksler did final and very thorough editing of the manuscript. For typing the final revised draft, Mr. Harish Bhatia is offered grateful thanks. He agreed at short notice, under trying circumstances, to type the full manuscript. Expert editing and proof correction by Mrs. Lila Weinberg of the University of Chicago Press helped considerably to improve the final product before it went into print. My grateful thanks to her.

Gratitude is extended also to the Committee on the Economy of China for its subsidy to the Research Center in Economic Development and Cultural Change toward the publication of this study.

Subramanian Swamy received his Ph.D. from Harvard University. He has taught economics at Harvard University and the Indian Institute of Technology at New Delhi, and is currently research professor at the Deen Dayal Research Institute, New Delhi. He is the author of *Indian Economic Planning: An Alternative Approach* and has contributed numerous articles to scholarly journals.